India's Festivals: A Treasure Trove of Folklore and Anecdotes

Mrs. Shubhra Varma
and
Dr. Anupam Varma

Qurate
quratebooks.com

India's Festivals: A Treasure Trove of Folklore and Anecdotes
Mrs. Shubhra Varma and Dr. Anupam Varma

Published in 2025

© Published by

Qurate Books Pvt. Ltd.
Goa 403523, India
www.quratebooks.com
Tel: 1800-210-6527, Email: info@quratebooks.com

ISBN: 978-93-58989-71-7

Dedicated with heartfelt gratitude to

Dr. Anupam Varma's parents

The Late Dr. Avadhesh Kanti Varma

& The Late Leela Varma

And

ShubhraVarma's parents

The Late Madan Mohan Saran Srivastava

& The Late Chandra Mukhi Srivastava

Acknowledgement

The idea of documenting the cherished stories surrounding India's festivals has been a long-standing ambition of ours. Through dedication and perseverance, we have successfully compiled and written these folklore and anecdotes. This endeavor would not have been possible without the support and contributions of many individuals and sources.

Our heartfelt gratitude goes to our children, Vaibhav, Manishi, and Nidhi, as well as our granddaughter, Kaashvi, who assisted us in every conceivable way. Kaashvi's expertise in handling IT requirements was particularly invaluable.

We are also grateful for the assistance provided by various AI platforms, including ChatGPT, Co-pilot, Gemini, and Google, especially for their role in generating images. The encouragement and support from our friends and relatives were crucial in motivating us to undertake this project.

Furthermore, we express our sincere thanks to the publishers for their unwavering cooperation.

Without the collective effort and support of all these individuals, the completion of this work would not have been possible. We deeply appreciate everyone's contributions.

Mrs. Shubhra Varma

Dr. Anupam Varma

Acknowledgement

Forward

The rich tapestry of India's cultural and spiritual heritage is intricately woven with stories, legends, and folklore passed down through generations. These narratives, rooted in ancient scriptures and mythology, form the bedrock of our vibrant festivals, customs, and traditions. In an era where globalization has blurred geographical boundaries, it becomes ever more crucial to preserve and share these stories with the younger generations, especially those of the Indian diaspora spread across the globe.

It is with great pleasure that I introduce India's Festivals: A Treasure Trove of Folklore and Anecdotes, a remarkable work jointly authored by my esteemed former colleague from BIMTECH, Greater Noida, Dr. Anupam Varma, who served as Deputy Director and Dean, Academics, and his wife, Mrs. Shubhra Varma. This book is a heartfelt endeavor to bring to light the mythological stories and cultural narratives that underpin the festivals celebrated by Indians, particularly those following the Hindu tradition.

While these stories originate from ancient religious texts, the authors have skillfully infused them with the richness of India's folk culture. They offer readers not just a retelling of age-old myths but a vibrant tapestry that reflects the diverse regional hues and nuances of our vast country. Each story is a journey into the heart of India's cultural consciousness, revealing how folklore and anecdote have shaped our understanding of the world and our place within it.

As an educationist and someone deeply invested in social, cultural, and educational issues, I recognize the profound value this book brings. For Indian families living abroad, it serves as a crucial link to their heritage, enabling parents to share the stories that are integral to our festivals with their children. These narratives not only educate but also foster a sense of identity and belonging, ensuring that cultural roots remain strong despite the distances.

The book delves into the mythological origins of various festivals, providing insights into their religious significance and the regional variations that make each celebration unique. For instance, the festival of Diwali is explored not just as the universally known "festival of lights" but through its myriad interpretations across different states, each adding a unique flavor to the collective celebration. This approach highlights the unity in diversity that is the hallmark of Indian culture.

What sets this book apart is its accessible and engaging storytelling style. The Varmas have managed to maintain the authenticity of the original tales while rendering them in a language that resonates with contemporary readers. The narratives are imbued with life, capturing the imagination of readers of all ages and making them ideal for family reading and discussions.

In today's fast-paced world, where traditions can sometimes be overshadowed by modernity, India's Folklore serves as a reminder of the timeless values and lessons embedded in our cultural narratives. The stories emphasize virtues such as resilience, justice, compassion, and the triumph of good over evil—principles that are universally relevant and essential in nurturing well-rounded individuals.

I commend Dr. Anupam Varma and Mrs. Shubhra Varma for their meticulous research and dedication in bringing this project to fruition. Their work fills a significant void for the Indian diaspora and anyone interested in delving deeper into India's rich cultural heritage. It is a testament to their commitment to education and cultural preservation.

As the Director General of IILM Lodhi Road, New Delhi, I have witnessed firsthand the trans-formative power of education in bridging cultural and generational gaps. Storytelling, in particular, is a powerful tool for imparting knowledge, values, and a sense of identity. This book harnesses that power effectively, making it a valuable resource for educators, parents, and cultural enthusiasts alike.

I wholeheartedly recommend India's Festivals: A Treasure Trove of Folklore and Anecdotes to anyone seeking to deepen their understanding of India's cultural and spiritual traditions. It is not merely a collection of stories but a gateway to the soul of India—a nation rich in diversity, history, and wisdom.

May this book inspire readers around the world to explore, cherish, and share the timeless tales that have shaped our culture and continue to enrich our lives.

Dr. Harivansh Chaturvedi
Director General, IILM Lodhi Road, New Delhi
November 2024

Preface

God is infinite,
God's stories are infinite.
They have been told and heard in countless ways
By saints and sages across the ages.

Storytelling in India has a timeless quality, rooted in the very origins of human expression. Long before writing existed, our ancestors used art, sculpture, and oral traditions to pass down their beliefs, values, and stories from one generation to the next. Through the delicate strokes of a brush or the skilled hands of a sculptor, the stories of gods, goddesses, and legendary heroes came to life. Temples and monuments like Ajanta, Ellora, Khajuraho, and Konark are not only architectural marvels but also visual narratives of India's mythological and historical richness. These carvings and frescoes depict divine beings, natural elements, and important historical events, preserving the stories that defined the collective consciousness of the time.

Over time, these stories transitioned from images on walls to words on palm leaves, as people began to write down what had been orally preserved. Through this evolution, stories continued to be a guiding force in shaping religion, morality, and community values. More than just folklore, they were embedded with profound wisdom and life lessons.

The festival calendar of India is a testament to this rich heritage of storytelling. Festivals have long been moments of joy, celebration, and devotion, but they also served as times for reflection and learning. Religious festivals, in particular, became occasions for elders to pass down the tales of gods and heroes to younger generations. After the customary Pooja (prayers) on such occasions, it was a tradition for the matriarchal in the household to gather everyone around and narrate the stories connected with the festival's origin and significance. Children listened with wide-eyed wonder, while adults deepened their understanding of the rituals and customs they had grown up with.

These stories did not follow the structured, question-and- answer format we are used to today. Instead, they flowed naturally, often inspired by the setting or event of the day. Elders were the natural keepers of these oral traditions, their storytelling skills honed over years of practice, drawing everyone in. Whether it was the story of Lord Rama's return to Ayodhya on Diwali, the tale of Prahlada's faith in Lord Vishnu during Holi, or the many legends of Lord Krishna associated with Janmashtami, these narratives served as vehicles for imparting values such as devotion, duty, and the triumph of good over evil.

Yet, in today's fast-paced world, many of these ancient stories and traditions are at risk of being lost. Modern life leaves little room for the slower, reflective moments that once allowed for the telling of these stories. The oral traditions that sustained them for centuries are disappearing, and with them, the cultural and spiritual heritage they embody.

The purpose of writing this book is to ensure that these valuable stories are not forgotten. This collection brings together ancient stories linked to India's vibrant festivals, arranged month by month. It is an attempt to rekindle the love for folklore and mythology, offering readers a chance to rediscover the wisdom hidden in these timeless tales. Each festival comes with its own set of stories that reveal a deeper significance, shedding light on the cultural, spiritual, and social practices that have sustained communities for generations.

We also expect this book to be of particular interest to the children who have been educated in English medium in India and abroad as it will give them an opportunity to know more about the Indian festivals and the stories associated with the same.

We hope this book not only serves as a valuable resource for those seeking to understand the stories behind India's festivals but also becomes a source of inspiration for all readers. These stories, though ancient, have a timeless appeal and continue to offer valuable lessons about life, faith, and community. In preserving them, we keep alive a treasure trove of wisdom, ensuring it remains accessible for future generations.

Shubhra Varma
Anupam Varma
February, 2025
NOIDA, India
E-mail: varma.anupam@gmail.com
Mobile No.: 9810137534, 9910180069

Contents

The Swastik: An Auspicious Symbol in Hindu Religion

The Swastik symbol, deeply revered in Hinduism and celebrated across numerous global cultures, carries profound meaning and spiritual significance. This emblem, a cross with arms bent at right angles, symbolizes auspiciousness, well-being, and positivity. The term "Swastik" originates from the Sanskrit svastika, a fusion of su (meaning "good") and asti (meaning "to be"), collectively signifying "well-being" or "auspiciousness." The Swastik's rich history, sacred symbolism, and pivotal role in Hindu rituals underscore its unique and influential presence.

The origins of the Swastik date back thousands of years, with evidence of its use found in ancient civilizations spanning India, China, Greece, Egypt, and beyond. The earliest known depictions of the Swastik appear in the Indus Valley Civilization, over 5,000 years ago. Within Hinduism, the Swastik holds a place of immense importance, symbolizing the harmony of the universe and the cyclical nature of existence, divinely orchestrated.

Globally, the Swastik has maintained its prominence as a revered symbol. In Hinduism, it is cherished as a divine emblem invoking blessings from deities and the cosmos. Similarly, in Buddhism and Jainism, it signifies peace, harmony, and equilibrium. Ancient cultures, including the Greeks, Romans, Celts, and Native Americans, adopted the Swastik as a representation of prosperity, fertility, and spirituality.

The Structure and symbolism of the Swastik in Hinduism.

In Hindu symbolism, the Swastik comprises a cross with four arms bent at right angles, typically oriented in a clockwise direction (referred to as the right-facing or Svastika). Each of these arms carries profound significance, often linked to the four Vedas—Rigveda, Yajurveda, Samaveda, and Atharvaveda—the foundational texts of Hindu spirituality. Additionally, the four arms are sometimes interpreted as representing the four purusharthas (objectives of human life) in Hindu philosophy: dharma (righteousness or duty), artha (wealth or prosperity), kama (desires or pleasures), and moksha (liberation or spiritual freedom).

In Hindu cosmology, the Swastik is also symbolic of the four cardinal directions—north, south, east, and west—reflecting the omnipresence of divine energy permeating every corner of the universe. It signifies the flow of positive energies from all directions, creating an environment devoid of negativity and conducive to meditation and spiritual practices.

Moreover, the four arms of the Swastik are associated with the four yugas (epochs) described in Hindu scriptures: Satya Yuga, Treta Yuga, Dvapara Yuga, and Kali Yuga. This association underscores the Swastik's connection to the concept of time, emphasizing the cyclical nature of existence and the Hindu belief in the eternal recurrence of cosmic ages.

The Importance of Swastik in Hindu Rituals and Daily Life

In Hindu rituals, the Swastik holds profound significance and is customarily inscribed at the commencement of religious ceremonies to sanctify the space and invoke divine blessings. Before initiating any auspicious occasion—such as a wedding, festival, or housewarming—the Swastik is drawn to seek the grace of the deities. Traditionally, this sacred symbol adorns doors, walls, and entrances, serving as a protective emblem that fosters prosperity and channels positive energy. It is believed that the Swastik purifies the environment, dispelling negative influences and creating a sanctified atmosphere.

The Swastik's association with Lord Ganesha, the elephant-headed deity of beginnings and remover of obstacles, is especially noteworthy. Often, the symbol is inscribed on objects or artifacts linked to his worship, amplifying the auspiciousness of his presence and invoking blessings for a new endeavor or a favorable outcome.

During the Hindu festival of Diwali, the Swastik takes on additional significance. It is commonly drawn with vermilion paste on cash registers, account books, or tools of trade, symbolizing a prayer for prosperity and success in the coming year. Its presence is intended to safeguard financial and personal pursuits from adversity, ensuring growth, success, and well-being.

Swastik in Spiritual Significance and Deeper Meanings

The Swastik carries profound spiritual significance in Hindu philosophy, embodying the dual aspects of divine energy—creation and destruction—working in harmony to sustain cosmic balance. This symbolism is often portrayed through its rotational form, representing the eternal cycle of birth, death, and rebirth. The clockwise or right-facing Swastik, predominantly used in Hindu worship, signifies the sun's journey across the sky, embodying the cyclical rhythm of life and nature's intrinsic harmony.

Conversely, the counterclockwise Swastik, or sauvastika, though less prevalent in Hinduism, bears its own distinct symbolism. Often associated with darker elements like destruction or chaos, it should not be perceived negatively. Rather, it signifies the destruction essential for renewal and regeneration. In certain Hindu rituals, this form is employed to symbolize the power to dispel evil forces and surmount challenges. Together, these dual forms of the Swastik underscore Hinduism's deep reverence for balance, emphasizing the belief that creation and destruction are inseparable and fundamental to the universal order.

The Swastik as a Tool for Meditation and Reflection

In Hindu spirituality, the Swastik stands as a profound emblem for meditation and introspection. Many practitioners focus on the Swastik as a means of attaining inner harmony and aligning themselves with the universal energy it symbolizes. Its symmetrical and balanced design fosters heightened focus and concentration, aiding in the quieting of the mind and the cultivation of inner tranquility. Consequently, the Swastik transcends its role as a symbol of external blessings and prosperity, evolving into a powerful tool for nurturing inner peace, wisdom, and spiritual clarity.

In Tantric traditions, the Swastik is revered as a yantra or mystical diagram employed in rituals and meditative practices, believed to channel cosmic energies effectively. Certain Hindu meditative techniques encourage the visualization of the Swastik to evoke a sense of protection, mental lucidity, and profound connection to the divine. Contemplating the Swastik is said to reveal deeper insights into the cycles of existence, the unity of dualities, and the intricate interconnectedness of all life forms.

The Swastik's Significance in Modern Times

In the modern world, the Swastik continues to hold great importance among Hindus and people of other faiths. Its presence is seen in Hindu temples, festivals, weddings, and even daily life as a reminder of hope, well-being, and the divine's pervasive presence. It has been adopted into various art forms, jewelry, and architecture, continuing to serve as a powerful reminder of cultural heritage and spiritual tradition.

The Swastik's Timeless Relevance

The Swastik, a sacred and powerful symbol in Hinduism, embodies a wealth of meanings—from harmony and well-being to the eternal cycles of creation. It stands as a testament to the deep spiritual insights and philosophies that form the foundation of Hindu culture. Despite its misrepresentation, the Swastik remains a revered emblem in Hinduism, celebrated for its beauty, depth, and ability to connect individuals with the divine.

For Hindus, the Swastik is not merely an ornament or design; it is a sacred symbol that invokes the divine's protection and blessings. It represents a connection with the past, a guide for the present, and hope for the future. Its timeless relevance is a reminder of the enduring power of symbols to inspire, protect, and uplift humanity in its journey through life.

Maas Chaturthi

Many tales surround the birth of Lord Ganesha and his rise to being the first god to be worshipped on the auspicious Chaturthi. Some of these stories are recounted below:

It is widely believed that Lord Ganesha was self-born. In her longing for a child, Goddess Parvati performed intense austerities and rituals. Pleased with her devotion, Ganesha appeared before her in the form of a Brahmin and asked, "Mother, what boon do you seek?" Parvati replied, "If you are truly pleased with me, grant me the blessing of a son." The Brahmin responded, "Enter your chambers; your son awaits you there."

When Parvati entered the room, she was overjoyed to see a radiant and healthy child lying peacefully on the bed. The air on Mount Kailash was filled with joy. Flowers rained from the heavens, and the gods arrived to offer their blessings to Parvati and her newborn son. However, one deity, Shani Dev, did not join the others. This displeased Parvati, and when she asked him why he did not come, Shani replied, "Mother, my gaze is inauspicious. I fear that harm may come to the child if I look upon him."

Parvati, however, insisted that Shani come to see her child. Reluctantly, Shani Dev entered the room. No sooner had his gaze fallen upon the infant than Ganesha's head was suddenly severed from his body. The joy on Kailash turned to chaos, and Parvati was inconsolable. Seeing her grief, Lord Shiva commanded his ganas (attendants) to search the world and bring him the head of any being whose mother was lying with her back to her child. After searching far and wide, the ganas returned with the head of an elephant calf. Using his divine powers, Shiva attached the elephant's head to Ganesha's body, restoring him to life. Blessed by all the gods, Ganesha grew wise and became known for his unmatched intellect.

Another version of Ganesha's birth is also popular: Once, while Lord Shiva went to bathe in the sacred Bhagwati River, Parvati was left alone at home. During this time, she created a child from the dust of her body and named him Ganesha. She instructed him to stand guard at the door and not let anyone enter.

When Shiva returned from his bath, he was unaware of this new child guarding the entrance. When Ganesha blocked his path, refusing him entry, Shiva's anger flared, and in a fit of rage, he severed Ganesha's head. Upon entering, he saw Parvati waiting for him with three plates of food. When asked about the extra plate, Parvati explained, "This is for our son, who is guarding the door." Realizing his mistake, Shiva immediately dispatched his ganas to bring back the head of an elephant, and thus, Ganesha was reborn with his new form, embodying divine wisdom.

Ganesha's intelligence was soon recognized by all the gods. One day, the gods approached Lord Shiva with a question: "Who among us shall be the first to be worshiped?" Shiva replied, "Whoever completes a full circumambulation of the universe and returns to me first will be given that honor."

All the gods mounted their vehicles and set off on the journey. Ganesha, however, used his brilliant mind. He simply circled his parents, Lord Shiva and Goddess Parvati, declaring them his universe. When the other gods returned from their long journeys, they were astonished to see mouse footprints around Shiva and Parvati. Upon hearing the story, they all agreed that Ganesha's wisdom and devotion made him the most worthy of being worshipped first.

There is yet another tale about Ganesha's precedence in worship: When Lord Vishnu was preparing for his wedding to Goddess Lakshmi, all the gods were invited to join the grand procession. However, they decided not to include Ganesha, as they feared that his insatiable appetite would cause embarrassment. They also mocked his large, round belly, his mouse vehicle, and his ladle-like ears, imagining that the women in attendance would laugh at his appearance.

As the wedding procession was about to begin, Narada, true to his nature, rushed to inform Ganesha of the gods' exclusion plan. Ganesha, in his calm wisdom, accepted it without protest. However, upon Narada's urging, Ganesha decided to intervene. He instructed his mice to dig up the ground from where Vishnu's chariot was to depart. When the time came, the chariot sank into the ground, unable to move.

Realizing their mistake, the gods rushed to Ganesha, humbly requesting his presence at the wedding. After much persuasion, Ganesha agreed to lead the procession, accompanied by Riddhi and Siddhi. From that day forward, it became tradition to worship Ganesha first before any auspicious event.

A Few Stories of Ganesha

Ganesha The Giver

There once lived an elderly blind woman with her son and daughter- in-law. Devoted to Lord Ganesha, the family prayed to him daily, seeking his blessings. One day, Lord Ganesha, moved by the old woman's devotion, appeared before her and said, "Mother, I am pleased with you. Ask for any boon you desire."

Being simple and unaware of what to request, the woman replied, "I will decide after speaking with my family and ask tomorrow."

When she returned home, she consulted her son, who advised her to ask for wealth. Her daughter-in-law, on the other hand, suggested requesting a grandson. Puzzled, the woman realized each person was only thinking of their own interests. She then approached herneighbor, who wisely suggested asking for her eyesight so she could see the world.

The next day, the old woman visited Lord Ganesha's temple again. When asked what she wished for, she said, "Lord, if you are truly pleased with me, grant me nine crore rupees, a strong and healthy body, the gift of eyesight, grandchildren, a godlike son-in-law, brothers and nephews, happiness for my entire family, and ultimately, salvation."

Lord Ganesha, amused by her clever request, smiled and said, "Mother, you have asked for many things, but I promised to grant you a boon, so all your wishes shall come true."

And so, the old woman received everything she asked for, and Lord Ganesha's blessings continued to shower upon her and all who believed in his grace.

Belief in Ganesha's Pooja

Ganesha's devotee, an old woman, would only eat after offering prayers. Once, she was making an idol of Ganesha andassoonasshepouredwateronit,theidolwouldmeltand merge with the earth. The old woman was confused abouthow to create and worship the idol of Ganesha.

While pondering on this, the old woman saw that the royal masons were building a temple for the king. She went tothem,leaningon acrutch,andrequestedthemto makeanidol of Ganesha for her so she could worship it daily.

The royal masons chased her away. After they chased her away, the old woman renounced food and water, saying that she would not eat or drink until she had a Ganesha idol. The royal masons told her that in the time taken to make your Ganesha ji, we will complete building this temple. Upon hearing this, the old woman returned home and lay down on her bed, but the royal masons were unable to complete the temple. No matter how hard they tried, the temple would collapse.

All the royal masons went to the king and explained their situation. The king asked them, "Did anyone come to you? And what were they saying?" "An old woman was asking us to make an idol of Ganesha, but we chased her away." The king said, "Find that old woman, no matter where she is." All the royal masons searched for the old woman everywhere. After traveling a long distance, they found the old woman lying in pain in a dilapidated hut. The people of the kingdom entered and brought the old woman to the king. The king asked about her suffering, and she explained her problem to the king. The king ordered his workers to first create an idol of Ganesha for the old woman so she could worship and drink water.

After doing this, the king's temple was built, and everyone started to worship Ganesha. Ganesha is easily pleased. If someone worships him with full faith, God fulfills their desires.

महिमा जासु जानि गणराऊ
प्रथम पूज्येत नाम प्रभाऊ

(Knowing his greatness,worship Ganesha. He is the first to be worshiped, his name is glorious.)

Ganesha and Kubera's Feast

Kubera, the god of wealth, was immensely proud of his riches. One day, in his arrogance, he decided to host a grand feast and invited Lord Shiva and Parvati to showcase his opulence. However, aware of Kubera's pride, Shiva and Parvati chose to send their young son, Ganesha, in their place.

Kubera was initially surprised but welcomed Ganesha with honor, eager to impress him. He served an extravagant meal, expecting to please the young deity. However, Ganesha's appetite seemed boundless. No matter how much food was brought before him, Ganesha demanded more, consuming everything with ease.

Eventually, Kubera's vast stores of food were depleted, yet Ganesha's hunger only grew stronger. In panic, Kubera fell to his knees, pleading for Ganesha's forgiveness and guidance.

With a gentle smile, Ganesha explained, "Kubera, the wealth of food alone cannot satisfy true hunger. Your pride in material wealth blinds you to the deeper values of humility and wisdom. To truly find satisfaction, you must approach Lord Shiva with humility and ask for blessings."

Humbled by the lesson, Kubera realized that his pride in his riches was shallow without wisdom and humility. This story highlights Ganesha's role as a teacher, reminding us that arrogance over wealth is meaningless. True fulfillment comes from understanding, humility, and seeking deeper truths.

Why Ganesha Has a Broken Tusk

A well-known story explains why Lord Ganesha is often depicted with a broken tusk. According to the Mahabharata, when the great sage Vyasa decided to compose this monumental epic, he sought Ganesha's help to be his scribe. Ganesha agreed but on one condition: Vyasa must dictate the verses without any pause. Vyasa, in turn, asked that Ganesha only write after fully comprehending each verse. This mutual agreement set the stage for the creation of one of the greatest epics in history.

As Vyasa began reciting, Ganesha diligently wrote down the verses. However, during the process, Ganesha's quill broke. Not wanting to disrupt the continuous flow of Vyasa's dictation or delay the monumental task, Ganesha quickly broke off one of his own tusks and used it to continue writing.

This act of breaking his own tusk reflects Ganesha's dedication to his duty and his selfless nature. Rather than interrupt the sacred work or ask for a replacement quill, Ganesha made a personal sacrifice to ensure that Vyasa's composition could proceed without delay. His broken tusk has since come to symbolize not only his resilience but also his willingness to sacrifice for the greater good.

In this way, Ganesha's broken tusk stands as a powerful symbol of sacrifice, selflessness, and dedication to the pursuit of knowledge. It is a reminder that true wisdom often requires personal sacrifice and unwavering commitment to one's responsibilities.

Ganesha's Guardianship of the Holy City of Kashi

In another legendary tale, Lord Ganesha plays a vital role in protecting the sacred city of Kashi (Varanasi), a place revered for its spiritual significance. The city was frequently under threat from marauding demons, who sought to desecrate its sanctity. To safeguard this holy land, Lord Shiva appointed Ganesha as its divine guardian, entrusting him with the responsibility of defending Kashi.

Whenever the demon hordes attempted to invade, Ganesha stood resolute, defeating them with a brilliant combination of wisdom and strength. His quick wit allowed him to outmaneuver his enemies, while his immense power ensured their downfall. No matter how formidable the opposition, Ganesha remained undefeated, protecting Kashi from harm and upholding the principles of dharma (righteousness).

Through his repeated victories, Ganesha not only preserved the sacredness of Kashi but also demonstrated his exceptional qualities as both a protector and a symbol of intellect. His ability to blend knowledge with might allowed him to serve the greater good, ensuring that virtue prevailed over evil.

This tale highlights Ganesha's dual nature as a wise defender and a powerful guardian. His role in safeguarding Kashi emphasizes how intellect and strength, when combined, can overcome even the greatest challenges, ensuring that righteousness triumphs over malevolence.

The Story of Ganesha and the Mouse

The story of Lord Ganesha and his mouse, Mushika, is a fascinating tale that explains why the mighty Ganesha rides a tiny mouse as his vehicle, or vahana. This legend carries deep symbolic meaning, representing humility, wisdom, and the power of transformation.

Once, there was a powerful and mischievous demon named Krauncha, originally a celestial musician (Gandharva) who had been cursed and transformed into a mouse due to his arrogance. In his new form, Krauncha grew to an enormous size and wreaked havoc wherever he went, destroying fields, homes, and temples, causing misery to all.

One day, Krauncha arrived at the ashram of Sage Parashar, where he continued his rampage, gnawing through everything in sight. The wise sage, witnessing the destruction, called upon Lord Ganesha for help.

When Ganesha arrived, Krauncha, still in his mouse form, charged at him, unaware of the lord's divine power. With calmness and wisdom, Ganesha quickly subdued him using his noose. Realizing he had been overpowered, Krauncha begged for forgiveness and asked to be freed from his curse.

Ganesha, ever compassionate, agreed but imposed one condition: Krauncha, now a mouse, must serve as his vehicle. Though initially worried about carrying Ganesha's large form, Ganesha assured him that with divine grace, he could bear the weight.

Thus, the mouse Krauncha, renamed Mushika, became Ganesha's loyal vahana, symbolizing that even the smallest beings can achieve great feats with divine blessings.

Symbolic Meaning

The pairing of Lord Ganesha and Mushika carries symbolic meanings:

1 **Conquering Ego:** The mouse represents desires, pride, and ego, which can often run wild if left unchecked. Ganesha, riding on the mouse, symbolizes control over these lower instincts and desires.

2 **Humility and Balance:** Despite his immense wisdom and power, Ganesha chooses a humble mouse as his vehicle, teaching us the value of humility and balance between power and modesty.

3. **Wisdom:** The small mouse can slip through the smallest of spaces, symbolizing that with wisdom, one can navigate through life's challenges with ease, regardless of their size or complexity.

Through this beautiful story, Lord Ganesha shows us how strength, wisdom, and humility can transform even the wildest challenges into tools for growth and learning

Pradosh Vrat: A Hindu Fast

Pradosh Vrat is a Hindu fast observed to please Lord Shiva. It is believed that observing this fast can grant devotees their desired wishes. This fast is performed on the fourteenth day of the waxing moon (Shukla Paksha) every month. The mention of this fast can also be found in the Shiva Purana.

Once, the gods and demons churned the cosmic ocean (Samudra Manthan) to obtain nectar (Amrita). During this churning, many valuable substances emerged, including the deadly poison, Halahala. This poison was so potent that it could destroy the entire universe. The gods and demons, fearing destruction, approached Lord Shiva to consume the poison and save the world. Shiva agreed and drank the poison, holding it in his throat, which turned blue.

The churning continued, and on the thirteenth day of the waxing moon, the nectar of immortality was obtained. Both the gods and demons thanked Shiva for his sacrifice.

The Tale of Pradosh Vrat

The Story of the Brahmin Woman and the Prince

In ancient times, a widowed Brahmin woman, along with her son, was struggling to make a living by begging in the forest. One day, while begging, they encountered a prince named Rajasuta, who had been exiled from his kingdom by his enemies. Moved by the prince's plight, the Brahmin woman brought him home and raised him as her own son, along with her biological son.

Around this time, a sage named Shandilya advised the Brahmin woman to observe the Pradosh Vrat and explained to her and her sons the greatness of Lord Shiva. Both sons and the widow began to perform this fast every month.

One day, while wandering in the forest, the two boys encountered a group of Gandharva maidens (celestial nymphs). The Brahmin woman's son returned home, but Rajasuta was captivated by their beauty and stayed with them. The Gandharva maidens, enchanted by Rajasuta's handsome appearance, sent their companions to fetch the rare Maulsari flower from a nearby forest. The prince revealed his identity as the son of the exiled king of Vidarbha.

The Wedding of Rajasuta and Anshumati

The Gandharva's Blessing

The Gandharva maiden, who had fallen in love with Rajasuta, told him, "I am the daughter of Vidarbha. I am skilled in music and dance. I have chosen you as my husband." She then placed a garland around his neck and told him to return in two days.

Rajasuta returned home and narrated the entire incident to his mother and brother, who were overjoyed.

Two days later, Rajasuta arrived at the appointed place in the forest. The Gandharva king, Anshumati's father, was already there. He revealed, "I visited Mount Kailash to find a suitable husband for my daughter. Lord Shiva revealed that there is a prince named Rajasuta, wandering without a kingdom. He is the perfect match for Anshumati. He has performed severe austerities to please me. I offer you my daughter and my celestial army to help you regain your lost kingdom. My daughter is worthy of you in every way. You will enjoy eternal happiness with her in this life and the afterlife."

Rajasuta and Anshumati were married. Rajasuta reclaimed his lost kingdom and upon his return, appointed his mother as the queen and his brother as the minister. It is believed that listening to this story during Pradosh Kal can lead to salvation (moksha).

Makar Sankranti

Makar Sankranti is one of the most significant festivals celebrated with immense joy across India and neighboring countries. What makes this festival unique is that it falls on the same date every year, usually between January 13th and 15th. According to the meteorological calendar, Makar Sankranti marks the transition when day and night are of equal length. From this day onward, the nights become shorter and the days longer, symbolizing the gradual arrival of warmer days and the end of winter's peak.

Makar Sankranti is celebrated in different forms throughout India, each region adding its own unique cultural touch to the festivities. In the northern states of Punjab and Haryana, the festival is known as Lohri. It is celebrated with great enthusiasm as people light bonfires, sing traditional songs, and rejoice in the harvest season's completion. The lighting of bonfires represents the warmth and energy of the Sun, and it is a way of bidding farewell to the long, cold nights.

In southern India, particularly in Tamil Nadu, the festival is known as Pongal. It is a celebration of the harvest, and people express gratitude to nature for providing sustenance. Similarly, in Assam, the festival takes the form of Bhogali Bihu, another harvest festival, where people come together to feast, sing, and dance. In Uttar Pradesh and several other northern states, the festival is celebrated as Makar Sankranti, with customs centered around food, charity, and prayers.

There is also a deep spiritual significance attached to Makar Sankranti. It is said that on this day, the Sun god, Surya, transitions from the Sagittarius constellation to Capricorn. This movement is symbolic of Lord Surya visiting his son Shani, the ruler of the Capricorn constellation. The day is considered auspicious for beginning new ventures and undertaking sacred rituals. In Rajasthan and Gujarat, kite flying is a major part of the celebrations, with the skies filled with colorful kites that represent joy and the cutting away of negativity.

In many regions, people bathe in sacred rivers like the Ganges and offer prayers to seek blessings. Khichdi, a simple and nutritious dish made from rice and lentils, is commonly eaten, and sweets made from sesame seeds, like tilgul and gajak, are prepared and shared among friends and family. The custom of giving and sharing food is an important aspect of the festival, emphasizing community spirit and compassion.

Makar Sankranti is also mentioned in ancient texts like the Mahabharata. It is said that Bhishma Pitamah, after being mortally wounded during the battle of Kurukshetra, chose to wait for the Sun to enter Uttarayana (the northward journey of the Sun) before relinquishing his life. He believed that those who died during this period would attain salvation and reach Vaikuntha (Heaven).

In Hindu mythology, Makar Sankranti also marks the day when Lord Vishnu vanquished demons and buried them under Mount Mandara, symbolizing the triumph of good over evil. The festival, therefore, not only celebrates the change in seasons but also the victory of righteousness and positivity over darkness and negativity.

Ganesh Chaturthi

Ganesh Chaturthi is also known as Sankashti Chaturthi. Mothers observe this fast to remove all the difficulties of their children.

A sister-in-law and her younger sister-in-law lived in a city with their respective families. The elder sister-in-law's house was full of happiness, prosperity, and wealth, while the younger sister-in-law was very poor. To support her family, the younger sister-in-law worked in the house of elder sister- in-law. The elder sister-in-law was proud of her wealth, but the younger sister-in-law, despite being poor, was simple and believed in fasting and worshiping God.

The festival of Ganesh Chaturthi arrived, but the younger sister-in-law had nothing to offer. She went to the forest and collected spinach, which she used to make prasad and observed the fast with devotion. At night, when the moon appeared, she performed the puja of Lord Ganesha with devotion. Pleased with her devotion, fast, and puja, Lord Ganesha knocked on her door. Seeing Lord Ganesha, the younger sister-in-law was overwhelmed. The Lord entered the house and said, "I am very hungry, give me something to eat." The sister-in-law was confused about what to offer to the Lord. She said, "Lord, you know everything. I am a poor woman, whatever I have cooked, please have it.

Ganesha accepted and ate the spinach Prasad. Ganesha was pleased. Now he said, "I will rest here for the night". The younger sister-in-law spread the best bedsheet she had, even though it was torn, on a bed and requested Ganesh ji to take rest. Ganesh ji had a deep sleep in the night and woke up at four in the morning. He said he wants to go to the toilet

The younger sister-in-law had cleaned the whole house and said, "Lord, you can go wherever you want." Ganesha was very pleased with her devotion. Wherever he went and did toilet, it all became gold.

The next day, the younger sister-in-law could not go to her elder sister-in-law's house for work. The younger sister-in-law became angry and sent her elder son to see why his aunt had not come to work. The child ran to his aunt's house and saw through the crack in the door that his aunt was collecting gold. Without entering, the child ran back to his mother and told her everything he saw. The elder sister-in-law became very envious and immediately went to her younger sister-in- law's house. The elder sister-in-law had never visited her sister-in-law's house before, so she was surprised to see her.

She asked her sister-in-law how she had become so rich overnight. The younger sister-in-law explained everything about her fast to her elder sister-in-law.

Due to greed, the elder sister-in-law also observed the fast, hid her wealth, and prepared spinach prasad. When Ganesha came to her house, she said, "I have nothing. This prasad is all I have. Please accept it. For Lord Ganesha She spread a torn old bedsheet on the charpai for him to rest. Early in the morning, when Ganesha expressed his desire to relieve himself, the younger sister-in-law told him to do it anywhere in the house. After a while, Ganesha disappeared. When morning came, they saw that the whole house was dirty. The neighbors came and heard the elder sister-in-law's story. Everyone said, "God is all-pervading."

One should worship God with a sincere heart to obtain their desired results.

Basant Panchami

When people are shivering due to the cold winter winds, the pleasant spring season arrives to soothe their minds. It is the birth of Goddess Saraswati, celebrated on the fifth day of the bright half of the month of Magh. It marks the beginning of a new season, which people celebrate with joy. Trees and plants start adorning themselves with new leaves.

On this day, Saraswati Puja is performed with great devotion, especially in Bengal. People often initiate their children's education on this day. White is the most beloved color of Goddess Saraswati, hence she is worshipped sitting on a white lotus, wearing white clothes, and adorned with a white garland. Her veena is also decorated with white. In Punjab, people enjoy flying kites.

In North India, people wear yellow clothes and make yellow items at home. Children take blessings from elders by greeting them. Goddess Saraswati bestows knowledge, long life, and intelligence, and brings prosperity everywhere

Some people also perform their ancestors' Pitar Tarpan.

Puranas describe Kamadeva dancing with the Sun God and Krishna dancing with Radha in Brajbhumi.

In 1916, Madan Mohan Malaviya established Banaras Hindu University on this day.

There is also a small story associated with Basant Panchami.

At the command of Lord Vishnu, Brahma Ji, the creator of the universe, began the divine task of creating the world. With his power, he formed the earth, the sky, the stars, and all living beings. However, after completing this grand creation, Brahma Ji decided to observe his handiwork and was disheartened by what he saw. The world, though physically beautiful, was silent and lifeless. The people were mute, the air was still, and there was no sound or joy to be found anywhere. The desolation and quietness filled Brahma Ji with sorrow.

In his sadness, Brahma Ji took his Kamandal (holy water pot) and sprinkled a few drops of water across the earth. Miraculously, the lifeless landscape began to transform. Lush greenery spread far and wide, and fields of golden-yellow mustard blossomed, filling the surroundings with vibrancy and beauty. Yet, something was still missing—the world remained silent.

As Brahma Ji pondered what to do, a radiant goddess suddenly appeared amidst the blooming mustard fields. She held a veena (a stringed musical instrument) in her hands, her presence exuding wisdom and grace. This divine goddess was Saraswati, the goddess of knowledge, music, and speech.

Brahma Ji, recognizing her divine power, approached her and requested, "Please, remove this silence from the world. Bless the people with the gift of speech and sound, so they may express themselves and live with joy."

In response, Saraswati Ji gracefully played her veena, and as the melodious notes echoed through the world, a miraculous change occurred. The people who had been mute suddenly found their voices, birds began to chirp, rivers flowed with music, and the world came alive with the sounds of life. It was as if the entire creation had found its soul through Saraswati Ji's veena.

Because she carries the veena, Saraswati Ji is also known as Veena Vadini and Veena Dharini, revered as the goddess who bestows wisdom, knowledge, and the power of speech.

On this auspicious day, it is also believed that the sacred river Ganges merged with the ocean, making it a highly auspicious time for bathing in the holy waters. Even today, devotees believe that taking a dip in the Ganges on this day washes away sins and brings blessings.

Thus, Saraswati Ji's divine intervention filled the world with knowledge, speech, and the beauty of sound, transforming it from a silent, desolate place into a vibrant, living creation.

Maha Shivratri

India, often called the land of festivals, celebrates its rich cultural heritage through a tapestry of religious and social observances. These festivals are deeply rooted in devotion, faith, and local traditions. One such significant festival is Maha Shivratri, celebrated with immense fervor across the country. According to the Hindu calendar, this auspicious day falls on the fourteenth night of the dark fortnight in the month of Phalgun (usually in February or March).

Maha Shivratri is believed to be the day when Lord Shiva, the god of destruction and transformation, married Goddess Parvati, the daughter of the Himalayas. According to legend, Shiva, adorned with ashes, surrounded by ghosts, demons, and sages, and wearing a garland of serpents, arrived at Parvati's home for their divine wedding. He carried a trident, bore the crescent moon on his head, and had the world-sustaining goddess on his forehead. This mystical night, marking the union of Shiva and Parvati, is celebrated as Shivratri, the "Night of Shiva."

On this sacred day, devotees fast, worship Lord Shiva, and offer him bell leaves, water, dhatura, fruits, and flowers. The central focus of worship is the Shiva lingam, a symbolic representation of Shiva's formless form. Women, especially married ones, observe the fast for the well-being of their husbands and marital bliss, while unmarried girls fast to seek a suitable husband. Those who do not have access to a Shiva lingam create one from wet clay, as it is believed to have the same spiritual significance.

The Shiva lingam itself has a deep connection to the festival. According to the Shiva Purana, it is said that the lingam appeared for the first time on this holy night. Brahma and Vishnu, who were in awe of its divine radiance, worshipped it, thus marking the beginning of the tradition of lingam worship.

An ancient story is tied to this festival, one that exemplifies Shiva's grace and his affection for all devotees, regardless of their social status. It is said that in ancient times, devotees would come to Lord Shiva, known as Shankar, seeking his blessings. One day, a devotee asked, "Lord, on which day and where can we mortals see you in the material world?" Shiva responded, "In the month of Phalgun, on the thirteenth and fourteenth days, I enter all Shiva lingams in the mortal world. Whoever offers bell leaves and water to my lingam and observes a fast will be blessed by me and have their wishes granted."

Hearing this, a poor man from the lower caste, a Mlechch living in Dinpur, decided to observe the fast and worship Shiva. He left his home and wandered into the forest but soon lost his way. As night fell, he climbed a bel tree for safety. Unbeknownst to him, a Shiva lingam rested beneath the tree. Throughout the night, he unknowingly dropped bell leaves and water onto the lingam, fulfilling the rituals of Maha Shivratri. His devotion, though unintended, pleased Shiva, who liberated him from his lower caste. In his next life, this man was reborn as Guha, the boatman who helped Lord Rama cross the Sarayu River.

This tale demonstrates Shiva's greatness—he is pleased by the sincere devotion of anyone who worships him with a pure heart and grants them their desired blessings.

Janki's Birth

First Story

On the ninth day of the Vaishakh month, Sita Ji was born in Virat Nagar, Nepal. It is said that Ravana sent his servants with pots filled with blood to bury them far away in the Virat Nagar. Once, during a famine in Virat Nagar, Janak Ji, along with his wife Sunaina, was ploughing the land. Their plough hit one of these pots, and a miraculous light emerged from the ground, revealing a young girl. Janak Ji brought her home and raised her like their own daughter. She was named as Sita, but being Janak ji's daughter was also called as Janki

As soon as Janaki was born, the famine ended, and heavy rains poured, bringing joy to the people. It is believed that on this day, one should observe a fast, bathe Sita Ji with holy water and offer her food after sunset. Janaki became the reason for Ravana's downfall.

Second Story

Sita has been revered by Indian women since ancient times, and her character has been considered exemplary. Goddess Parvati blessed Sita with eternal marital bliss, saying, "May your husband always be devoted to you."

This was the Treta Yuga era, a time when people possessed extraordinary powers, capable of transforming their entire personalities in the blink of an eye. In the Mithila kingdom, King Janak ruled, and his wife, Sunaina, was a pious queen. Despite enjoying all kinds of luxuries, they were saddened by their childlessness. The kingdom faced a famine, and the people suffered from hunger and thirst. Upon the king's orders, a tunnel was dug to bring water, providing relief to the people. Witnessing the people's happiness, the king and queen were satisfied, but the pain of childlessness persisted.

The king summoned the royal guru and sought advice. The guru advised the king to renounce his royal life and perform penance for seven days. The king followed his advice. Following the guru's advice, the king, accompanied by sages chanting Vedic hymns, began to dig the earth with a golden shovel. Queen Sunayana was also present.

Suddenly, the shovel hit an iron box, which opened, revealing a beautiful baby girl inside. King Janak, delighted, handed the baby to Sunayana, and thus, Janaki, the daughter of Janak, was born. This happened in Virat Nagar, Nepal. In honor of the Earth Goddess, the baby was named Sita. Sita, with her playful antics, brought immense joy to her parents.

After a while, Sita's younger sister, Urmila, was born. Both sisters loved listening to stories of their ancestors from their nanny. The nanny also told them about a magical bow belonging to Lord Shiva, which had been kept in a locked room since their grandfather's time. No one was allowed to enter that room.

One day, while playing in the palace, the sisters' ball rolled into that forbidden room. Sita, seeing the ball, moved the bow and retrieved the ball. The nanny, who was following them, was astonished and informed Sunayana. Many people tried to move the bow, but it wouldn't budge. King Janak then vowed that whoever could break the bow would marry Sita. Sita, Urmila, and their cousins, Shrutikirti and Mandavi, were all present. They would all play and fill the palace with her laughter.

Gradually, these four sisters reached adulthood. Sita was interested in studying historical texts. She was deeply influenced by the lives of Sati Anasuya, Savitri Satyavan, Gargī, and Bhūdevi. Shrutīkirti was interested in the art of singing, Urmila excelled in dance, while Māndavī was fascinated by art.

Once, Vishvāmitra visited Janaka's royal court and expressed concern about the terror of demons in the forest. Upon hearing this, Janaka was saddened and sent Vishvāmitra to Ayodhyā to request Rāma and Laksmana to go to the forest. Initially, Daśarath was hesitant, but upon persuasion, he sent Rāma and Laksmana to complete their religious duties.

Sītā would regularly receive news of Rāma Chandra's valor and heroism, and in her heart, she began to consider him her husband.

When Sita reached marriageable age, Janaka announced a competition throughout the kingdom. The brave warrior who could break the bow would win Sita's hand in marriage. Many warriors and heroes participated, but none could even move the bow. Rāma and Lakṣmaṇa, who were returning from the forest, were also invited to the competition.

With Vishvāmitra's blessings, Rāma approached the bow, bowed to it, and effortlessly broke it. The entire gathering erupted in joy, and Sītā, garlanded with flowers, accepted Rāma as her husband. "At the time of farewell, Sita's parents, birds, and animals were all saddened. Her mother blessed Sita and gave her appropriate advice.

'Sita, you are Rama's strength. Be his support in times of sorrow. Bring him happiness and be his companion in joy and sorrow. Always remember that the people of Ayodhya and its kingdom are your own. It is your duty to uphold their customs and traditions. Respect them more than your own life.' With her mother's blessings, Janaki embarked on a new journey and always followed her mother's advice.

According to one legend, Sita's birthplace is believed to be Janakpur in Nepal. It was here that Rama and Sita were married. There is a place called Dhanushdham in Janakpur, where Lord Rama broke the bow. Its remnants are still worshipped today.

According to another legend, Sita was born in a place called Sita Madhi in Bihar. After Sita's marriage, Janaka built a pond known as Janaki Kund. The idols of Rama, Lakshmana, and Sita were installed in this pond."

Sita Ji is addressed by various names. Due to being Janaka Ji's daughter, she is called 'Janaki.' As she was born from the Earth, she is called 'Sita.' Being a princess of Mithila, she is also known as 'Maithili.' And as she is the other half of Lord Rama, she is also called 'Rāma.'

Holika's Story

Once upon a time, in the Satya Yuga, there lived a powerful and arrogant demon king named Hiranyakashyap. His reign was marked by terror and cruelty, and he considered himself invincible due to a boon he had received, which made him immune to death under specific conditions. His son, Prahlad, was the exact opposite—a devout and steadfast worshipper of Lord Vishnu. Despite Hiranyakashyap's hatred for Vishnu, Prahlad remained devoted, much to his father's dismay.

Hiranyakashyap could not tolerate his son's devotion to Vishnu, whom he considered his greatest enemy. In his fury, he devised numerous ways to kill Prahlad, but divine grace protected the boy every time. He threw Prahlad off a mountain, but the young devotee emerged unscathed. He was cast into a pit of venomous snakes, yet they did not harm him. He was even placed under the feet of a wild elephant, but again, Prahlad remained unharmed. No matter how cruel the attempts, Prahlad's unwavering faith in Lord Vishnu shielded him from all harm.

Frustrated and desperate, Hiranyakashyap summoned his sister Holika, who had a boon that made her immune to fire as long as she wore a divine shawl. Hiranyakashyap ordered her to take Prahlad into a burning fire, believing that her invincibility would allow her to burn Prahlad to death. Holika, blinded by her brother's commands, agreed to the wicked plan. She sat in the blazing fire with Prahlad in her lap, draped in her magical shawl.

However, Holika had forgotten a crucial condition of her boon—it would only protect her if she used it for good, not for evil. As the flames rose, divine intervention occurred. The shawl flew off Holika and wrapped itself around Prahlad, shielding him from the fire. Holika, consumed by the flames, perished, while Prahlad emerged unharmed, his faith in Vishnu even stronger.

This miraculous event enraged Hiranyakashyap further. In his fury, he asked Prahlad, "Where is your God now?" Calmly, Prahlad replied, "He is everywhere—in this pillar, above, below, and all around." Enraged by this, Hiranyakashyap struck a pillar with his sword. At that very moment, Lord Narasimha, a fierce avatar of Vishnu, appeared from the pillar, taking the form of a half-lion, half-man. He seized Hiranyakashyap and killed him at the threshold of his palace, neither inside nor outside, thus fulfilling the conditions of the demon's boon.

Since that day, Holika Dahan is celebrated every year to symbolize the triumph of good over evil. The next day, people rejoice and celebrate the festival of Holi, marking the victory of righteousness with color, joy, and enthusiasm.

Sheetala Ashtami

Sheetala Ashtami holds a special significance in Hindu culture, celebrated with great devotion and faith. Observed on the seventh day after Holi, in the month of Chaitra, this festival is dedicated to Sheetala Mata, a revered goddess believed to ward off diseases such as smallpox, measles, and skin infections. One of the unique aspects of this festival is that devotees observe a fast and consume only stale food, offering the same as prasad (sacred food) to Sheetala Mata. This practice gives the festival its name—Sheetala Ashtami, with "Sheetala" meaning coolness or calm, and "Ashtami" referring to the eighth day of the lunar month.

According to the Skanda Purana, Sheetala Mata was created by Lord Brahma and is considered a manifestation of Goddess Parvati. Worshiping her is believed to bring relief from various ailments and epidemics. Devotees believe that by observing this fast and seeking Sheetala Mata's blessings, their families will be protected from illness and other misfortunes.

Sheetala Ashtami is celebrated with great enthusiasm in regions like Jodhpur and Jaipur in Rajasthan, as well as in West Bengal, Nepal, Bangladesh, and parts of Pakistan. Markets come alive with festive decorations, and in rural areas, animals are adorned in colorful attire and sold in vibrant markets. This festival creates a sense of joy and community as people come together to honor the goddess.

An integral part of the celebrations is the recitation of the *Sheetala Ashtak,* a hymn composed by Lord Shiva to praise the greatness of Sheetala Mata. This ancient chant is recited by devotees after performing puja, and it is believed to invoke the goddess's blessings and protection. The hymn begins with these lines:

"Vande 'ham śītala devī rās bhasthāṃ digambaraṃ bhārjanī kal śopatăṃ sūrpā lankṛta mastakām"

There is a popular story that highlights the importance of this fast. In a certain kingdom, an old woman was known for her unwavering devotion to Sheetala Mata. One night, a terrible fire broke out in the kingdom, destroying everything in its path. Amidst the chaos, the king noticed that the old woman's house was miraculously untouched by the flames. Astonished, the king summoned her and asked how her home had been spared from such devastation.

The old woman humbly replied, "Maharaj, I have been observing the Sheetala Mata fast every year. It is by her grace that my house was saved from the fire."

Upon hearing this, the king was filled with faith and immediately decreed that all his subjects should observe the Sheetala Ashtami fast, believing that if the old woman had been blessed by Sheetala Mata, others too could receive her divine protection. From that day onward, the festival gained even greater prominence, symbolizing the power of faith and the protective grace of Sheetala Mata.

Nav-ratri

Navratri, one of the most significant festivals in Hinduism, is celebrated during the bright half of the Chaitra month, marking the transition from winter to spring. This nine-day festival is devoted to the worship of Goddess Durga in her various forms, symbolizing the triumph of good over evil and the divine feminine's nurturing yet powerful nature. The word "Navratri" itself means "nine nights," during which devotees engage in fasting, prayer, and rituals to honor the goddess.

The first day of Navratri holds special importance as it marks the beginning of the Hindu New Year. According to ancient belief, this is the day when Lord Brahma, the creator of the universe, is said to have created the Earth. Hence, Navratri is not only a religious festival but also a celebration of renewal, both of nature and the self. Observing a fast during Navratri is believed to cleanse the body, sharpen the mind, and strengthen spiritual energy. This period of fasting helps devotees control their senses, enhance their willpower, and cultivate positive thinking.

The festival also symbolizes the first harvest of the world. Many devotees plant seeds on the first day of Navratri and nurture them throughout the nine days, signifying growth and prosperity. One of the most symbolic elements in Navratri rituals is the coconut, which is considered sacred in Hinduism. The coconut's hard outer shell represents the ego and pride that human beings often carry, while the sweet, nourishing fruit inside symbolizes the pure and divine nature within all of us. Just as one must break the shell to reach the fruit, so too must we break our ego to experience true inner joy and enlightenment.

The web of fibers surrounding the coconut's shell represents the many vices of human nature, such as jealousy, hatred, selfishness, and delusion. Shedding these vices is essential for living a fulfilling and meaningful life, a lesson underscored throughout the festival of Navratri.

During these nine days, nine different forms of Goddess Durga are worshipped, each representing a unique aspect of the divine feminine energy. These forms are:

- Mahākālī: The fierce and powerful goddess who destroys evil.
- Māhālāksmī: The goddess of wealth and prosperity.
- Cāmundā: The slayer of demons.
- Yogamāyā: The divine illusion, representing the power of creation.

- Raktādantīkā: The goddess who controls anger.
- Śākumbharī: The nurturing mother, who provides food and sustenance.
- Bhramārī Devī: The goddess of the bees, symbolizing protection.
- Chandikā: The goddess of fierce power and strength.
- Durgā: The ultimate form of the goddess, the embodiment of power and protection.

Each day of Navratri is dedicated to one of these forms of Durga, and the worship of these goddesses signifies the progression from darkness to light, from ignorance to wisdom, and from negativity to positivity.

The last day of Navratri, known as Ashtami or Durga Ashtami, is especially significant. On this day, devotees undertake a fast, and it is traditional to honor young girls, known as "Kanya Puja," who are seen as representations of the goddess herself. After offering them food and gifts, the fast is broken, symbolizing the completion of the spiritual journey undertaken during the festival.

Navratri is thus a celebration of inner transformation, spiritual growth, and the divine feminine's immense power, all while rejoicing in nature's rebirth.

Rama Navami

Thousands of years ago, when only a few Hindu festivals were celebrated, Rama Navami stood out as one of the most significant. Celebrated on the ninth day of the bright half of the Chaitra month, this auspicious day marks the birth of Lord Rama, an incarnation of Lord Vishnu, who is revered as the embodiment of dharma (righteousness) and virtue. It is believed that whenever evil forces attempt to dominate and disturb the cosmic balance,

God incarnates in human form to restore harmony and alleviate suffering. Lord Rama's birth was one such divine intervention to combat the tyranny of the demon king Ravana and to establish righteousness.

Rama Navami is celebrated not only in India but also in other countries with significant Hindu populations. Devotees observe this day with great devotion, and it is widely believed that those who fast on Rama Navami are blessed with infinite happiness and spiritual fulfillment. The story of Lord Rama's birth, narrated in the epic Ramayana, is at the heart of this celebration and continues to inspire people across generations.

According to the Ramayana, King Dasharatha of Ayodhya had three wives: Kaushalya, Kaikeyi, and Sumitra. Despite their deep desire for children, none of them had been able to conceive, leaving the king deeply distressed. Seeking divine intervention, he prayed to the gods for guidance. The gods advised him to visit Lord Vishnu, the protector of the universe, for a solution. Hearing King Dasharatha's plea, Lord Vishnu decided to incarnate as his son to bring an end to the rising forces of evil.

At the advice of Sage Vashishtha, the king performed a special ritual known as the Putra Kameshti Yagna to obtain a child. During the yagna, Yagneshwar, the lord of sacrifices, appeared with a bowl of sacred kheer (sweet rice pudding). King Dasharatha distributed the kheer among his three wives. Soon after, Kaushalya conceived Lord Rama, who represented righteousness and virtue. Kaikeyi gave birth to Bharat, believed to be the origin of the name 'Bharat,' and Sumitra conceived Lakshmana and Shatrughna. Each of these sons was blessed with a portion of Vishnu's divine energy, and together they would later play crucial roles in the Ramayana.

When Lord Rama was born, he initially appeared in his divine form. Kaushalya, overwhelmed by his divinity, requested him to assume a more human appearance and enjoy the bliss of childhood. Rama obliged, and his naming ceremony, along with that of his brothers, took place eleven days later. The princes were then educated in the gurukul, where they excelled in various disciplines, preparing them for the challenges they would face in the future.

Rama Navami is unique in that, during a time when caste discrimination was prevalent, even Shudras (those considered of lower caste) were allowed to celebrate this festival, emphasizing the inclusivity and righteousness of Lord Rama's rule.

Additionally, the festival of Hanuman Jayanti, celebrated on the fourteenth day of Chaitra, marks the birth of Lord Hanuman, who is considered an incarnation of Lord Shiva. Hanuman was born to assist Lord Rama in his quest, and his devotion to Rama is legendary. Pleasing Hanuman Ji is said to please Lord Rama, as their bond of loyalty and service is unparalleled in Hindu mythology.

Hanuman Jayanti

Lord Hanuman is a multifaceted personality whose equal cannot be found anywhere else. He is humble, dignified, compassionate, skilled in behavior, and an all-powerful deity. He is the most devoted devotee of Lord Rama, who once said about

Hanuman, "You embody all the four castes: Brahmin, Kshatriya, Vaishya, and Shudra." When Hanuman asked why he was categorized as a Vaishya, Rama replied, "You have served me so much that I cannot repay your debt."

The story of Hanuman's birth is very interesting. Once, the sage Angera went to Indra. To honor him, Indra asked Punjikasthala, a celestial dancer, to perform a dance. Sage Angera was not interested in watching the dance and instead closed his eyes and focused on meditating on his deity. After the dance, Indra asked Angera how he found the performance. Angera truthfully replied that he was engrossed in meditation and did not see the dance. Punjikasthala became very angry and insulted the sage. Angera initially listened patiently but then became enraged and cursed her, saying that she would have to be born on Earth as a monkey. The frightened celestial maiden sought forgiveness.

The sage felt pity for her and said, "You will have to go to Earth, but you will give birth to a devotee of the Supreme Being who will possess all virtues. You will be born as a woman, but if you look at any man with love, you will transform into a monkey."

On Mount Sumeru, Anjana, the daughter of the wind god Vayu, gave birth to Hanuman. He spent his childhood playing in the forests around the mountain. During his youth, the monkey king Kesari came to the forest to hunt. As soon as Anjana saw him, she fell in love and started crying. Kesari, who was also a monkey, approached her and asked why she was crying. Anjana confessed her love for him, and Kesari agreed to marry her.

After some time, Anjana performed a yagya to have a child. During the ritual, she chanted praises to Shiva. Legend has it that while she was performing the ritual, a hawk flew by and dropped a bowl of kheer (rice pudding) into her lap. This kheer was the same one that Dasharatha had offered to his wife Kausalya before the birth of Rama. Believing it to be a blessing from Shiva, Anjana consumed the kheer. Shiva himself wished to come to Earth to serve Lord Rama.

Thus, on the full moon night of Chaitra Shukla Paksha, Hanuman was born with the blessings of four divine beings:

Angera Rishi's curse and blessings, Lord Shiva's blessings, Yagya performed to hava a child, and Vayu Devta's (wind god) blessings.

Hanuman Ji is known by various names, including Pavana Putra, Mahavir, Anjaneya, Sankat Mochan, and Bajrang Bali. He is always devoted to Lord Rama and is dedicated to serving him and fulfilling his tasks. With his exceptional strength and intelligence, he can accomplish even the most difficult tasks with ease.

Whether it's fetching Sanjivani herb, burning Lanka, or crossing the ocean, Hanuman Ji is always ready to serve Lord Rama with complete devotion. He is the eleventh Rudra avatar of Lord Shiva.

Hanuman Jayanti is a significant festival for wrestlers and those involved in sports. Many competitions are held on this day. Hanuman Ji's photo is displayed, and the festival begins with the chant of "Jai Bajrang Bali." Hanuman Ji's power is never used for negative purposes.

This festival is celebrated one day earlier in Maharashtra compared to North India. In North India, people observe a fast on this day and recite Hanuman Chalisa to seek blessings and protection from evil spirits. Hanuman Ji is present in almost all temples in North India.

In many Indian homes, you can find images of Hanuman Ji displayed and worshipped. In Mauritius, it's common to see Hanuman Ji statues in front of Hindu homes. From a distance, you can spot the yellow flag associated with Hanuman Ji.

I have attempted to capture some interesting anecdotes from Hanuman Ji's childhood.

Once, while playing, Hanuman Ji mistook the bright red sun for a ripe fruit and tried to eat it. Indra, the god of thunder, intervened by striking Hanuman Ji's jaw with lightning. This incident led to Hanuman Ji being called "Hanu," which means "distorted jaw," and "Man," meaning "human."

Hanuman Ji aspired to be a disciple of Surya Bhagwan (Sun God) and expressed his desire to learn from him. Surya Bhagwan, always on the move, replied that he didn't have time. Hanuman Ji then assumed his divine form, placing one foot in the east and the other in the west, and said, "Now I am always in front of you. Please teach me." Impressed, Surya Bhagwan accepted Hanuman Ji as his disciple.

As a child, Hanuman Ji was known to trouble sages who were meditating. As a result, a sage cursed him, saying that he would forget his strength unless someone reminded him of it. When it was time to cross the ocean to find Sita, Jamvant reminded Hanuman Ji of his immense power.

Once, while watching Sita Ji apply vermilion (sindoor) to her forehead, Hanuman Ji asked her why she did it. Sita Ji replied that it was a symbol of her marital status and brought joy to Lord Rama. Without understanding the significance, Hanuman Ji applied vermilion all over his body. Today, Hanuman Ji's idols are adorned with yellow vermilion.

When Lord Rama was about to ascend to heaven, he asked his followers to accompany him. Many followed him, but Hanuman Ji declined, stating that he would remain on Earth as long as people remembered and chanted his name with devotion. Even today, it is believed that Hanuman Ji is the first to arrive and the last to leave at places where Rama Katha (stories of Rama) are recited.

Once, Lord Rama was distributing pearl necklaces as gifts. Hanuman Ji, seeing the pearls, started breaking them one by one. When questioned about his actions, Hanuman Ji revealed that he was observing Rama's image within each pearl. He believed that if Rama was not present in his life, these pearls held no value for him. Hanuman Ji's selfless devotion and unwavering faith in Rama are truly inspiring

On Hanuman Jayanti, we celebrate his selfless service and remember his extraordinary personality as an ideal to follow.

"Keep chanting the Lord's name and make wishes.

Hanuman Ji shows the way to reach Lord Rama.

Akshaya Tritiya

In ancient times, Hindus placed great importance on selecting auspicious moments for any significant undertaking. Akshaya Tritiya is one such day, considered extremely auspicious for embarking on new ventures, conducting religious ceremonies, or making important life decisions. Whether it's a marriage, starting a new business, purchasing property, or setting off on a long journey, doing so on Akshaya Tritiya is believed to ensure success and lasting prosperity.

The word "Akshaya" means "never-ending" or "imperishable," symbolizing eternal prosperity, abundance, and success. This festival occurs on the third day of the bright half of the Hindu month of Vaisakha (April-May). It is unique because the sun and the moon are both believed to be at their brightest on this day, and many also consider it to mark the beginning of the Satya Yuga, the golden age of truth and righteousness.

Akshaya Tritiya is also linked to several important events in Hindu mythology. It is celebrated as the birth anniversary of Lord Parshuram, the sixth avatar of Lord Vishnu, known for his courage and righteousness. Furthermore, it is said that on this very day, the great epic *Mahabharata* was first narrated by Sage Vyasa and written by Lord Ganesha, marking the start of one of the most revered texts in Hinduism.

One of the most well-known stories associated with Akshaya Tritiya is that of the Pandavas during their exile. During this time, they were gifted the divine *Akshaya Patra* by Lord Krishna. This miraculous vessel had the ability to provide an endless supply of food, ensuring the Pandavas and their followers were never hungry, no matter how long their exile lasted. The *Akshaya Patra* symbolizes abundance and the idea that those who perform righteous deeds with devotion will always be taken care of by the divine.

Another beloved tale connected to Akshaya Tritiya is the story of Lord Krishna and his childhood friend, Sudama. Sudama, a poor Brahmin, was living in extreme poverty and decided to visit Krishna, who was then the king of Dwaraka, to seek assistance. Carrying with him only a humble offering of puffed rice, Sudama hesitated to ask for help and instead enjoyed Krishna's warm hospitality. Krishna, delighted to see his old friend, treated Sudama with the utmost respect, washing his feet and honoring him with great reverence, exemplifying the principle of "Atithi Devo Bhava"—the guest is God.

Though Sudama never voiced his needs, upon returning home, he discovered that his modest dwelling had been transformed into a magnificent palace, and his family was adorned in fine clothes and enjoying great wealth. Krishna had silently bestowed this blessing on him, demonstrating his boundless grace. The story of Krishna and Sudama teaches that humility, friendship, and devotion can yield rewards beyond measure, and that true wealth lies in divine connection and contentment.

In the regions of Rajasthan and Gujarat, Akshaya Tritiya is also celebrated as "Akha Teej." On this day, people take ritual baths in holy rivers, offer prayers to Lord Ganesha and Goddess Lakshmi, and purchase gold, which is believed to bring prosperity and wealth. Buying gold on Akshaya Tritiya is particularly significant, as gold represents wealth that never diminishes, aligning with the symbolism of the day.

Additionally, Akshaya Tritiya is notable for the births of many important figures in Indian spirituality, including Lord

Buddha, Ramanujacharya, Adi Shankaracharya, and Swami Chinmayananda. These revered saints and teachers contributed greatly to India's spiritual heritage and are remembered for their profound teachings on the path of enlightenment.

In essence, Akshaya Tritiya is a day of limitless potential, a day when divine blessings flow abundantly, ensuring success, prosperity, and joy in all endeavors undertaken with faith and devotion.

Baisakhi

After months of hard work in the winter, farmers are filled with joy when they bring home their abundant harvest. This festival, Baisakhi, falls on April 13th or 14th, marking the arrival of the Rabi crop. People celebrate with dancing, singing, and gatherings to rejoice in their achievements.

On April 13, 1699, Guru Gobind Singh, the tenth Sikh Guru, summoned a large gathering at Anandpur Sahib. He announced that he would choose his successor and sought a volunteer to lay down their life for the community. An audience of about 50000 people became fully quite. On repeating this announcement many times, amidst the silence, a man named Daya Ram Khatri from Lahore stepped forward, ready to sacrifice his life. Guru Gobind Singh took him to his private chamber, and the people witnessed a stream of blood flowing out. The sight of blood flowing from the chamber filled everyone with awe and wonder.

The Khalsa Tradition

After the Sikh Guru, Guru Gobind Singh, again announced that he wants head, Dharamdas Jat stepped forward and entered the private chamber. Following him, a dhobi named Makhan Chand from Dwarka entered, then a barber from Bidar, Karnataka, and finally, Hemant Rai, a water carrier from Puri. One by one, these five individuals entered the chamber. The people in the gathering thought that these five persons have been sacrificed at the feet of God. Then the Guru along with these five people emerged, symbolizing their dedication and willingness to sacrifice their lives for the Guru. The people watching were deeply moved by their unwavering devotion and believed that they had attained spiritual enlightenment.

Guru Gobind Singh appeared on the stage with these five individuals, known as the "Panj Pyare" (Five Beloved), and announced the establishment of the Khalsa tradition. He introduced new customs, such as carrying a sword in front of men and a kaur (comb) in front of women. A large steel container filled with water and sugar was prepared, and Mata Sundari sprinkled this holy water on everyone present, symbolizing the baptism of the Khalsa. This tradition of distributing sharbat (sweetened drink) continues to be practiced during Sikh festivals.

The Khalsa tradition established certain principles and guidelines. The power and strength of the Khalsa should be used for good deeds. There should be only one Guru and one holy book (Sri Guru Granth Sahib). Both men and women are equal in the eyes of the Khalsa faith. Before taking any action, one should contemplate their motives, the purpose behind their actions, and the potential benefits for humanity.

Bat Savitri

Bat Savitri is a traditional Hindu festival celebrated by married women on the new moon day of the month of Jyaistha (May-June). The festival is dedicated to the banyan tree, a symbol of longevity and steadfastness, and is observed with fasting and rituals to ensure the well-being and long life of their husbands.

The core of this festival is the story of Savitri, a woman known for her unwavering devotion to her husband, Satyavan, and her triumph over death through the strength of her love and piety.

On the day of Bat Savitri, women gather at a banyan tree and perform rituals that include wrapping raw cotton thread around its trunk while circumambulating it in reverence. The banyan tree is a symbol of shelter, stability, and resilience—qualities that are celebrated in this festival. While performing the rituals, women tell and listen to stories of Savitri, drawing inspiration from her devotion. One of the most cherished stories narrated on this day goes as follows:

In the ancient kingdom of Bhadra Desh, there lived a wise and righteous king named Ashwapati. He had a beautiful and virtuous daughter named Savitri. As Savitri reached the age of marriage, she heard of a noble young man named Satyavan, who lived in the forest and was known for his strength and virtue. Despite knowing that Satyavan had lost his kingdom and was living in poverty with his blind parents, Savitri was determined to marry him. Her father, concerned for her happiness, consulted the sage Narada, who revealed a tragic truth: Satyavan had only one year left to live.

Despite this knowledge, Savitri remained resolute in her decision. She left behind her royal life, wealth, and comfort to live with Satyavan and his family in the forest. There, she devoted herself to serving her blind parents-in-law with unwavering dedication. As the time of Satyavan's predicted death approached, Savitri increased her prayers and fasting. On the fateful day, when Satyavan went into the forest to cut wood, Savitri followed him, as instructed by her parents-in-law.

When the appointed hour of Satyavan's death arrived, he collapsed in the forest, his head resting in Savitri's lap. At that moment, Lord Yama, the god of death, appeared to claim Satyavan's soul. Savitri, however, would not let go so easily. She followed Yama, pleading with him to spare her husband's life. Moved by her devotion, Yama offered her three wishes—on the condition that she would not ask for Satyavan's life.

For her first wish, Savitri asked for her parents-in-law's

eyesight to be restored, and Yama granted it. For her second wish, she asked for her father-in-law's lost kingdom to be returned to him. Yama granted this too. Despite these blessings, Savitri continued to follow Yama. Surprised, Yama asked why she persisted. Savitri replied that as a devoted wife, it was her duty to stay with her husband, even in death.

Impressed by her persistence and loyalty, Yama granted her a third wish. This time, Savitri cleverly asked for 200 sons. Yama, bound by his promise, granted the wish. But Savitri pointed out that as he had taken her husband away, she could not fulfill her wish for sons. Realizing he had been outwitted, Yama relented and returned Satyavan's soul to his body, bringing him back to life.

In gratitude, Savitri went to the banyan tree, worshipped it as instructed by Goddess Parvati, and brought her husband back to life. Since that day, women celebrate Bat Savitri by worshipping the banyan tree, praying for their husbands' long lives, and drawing inspiration from Savitri's devotion, love, and wisdom. The festival highlights the values of loyalty, devotion, and the power of a woman's determination in overcoming even the greatest of challenges.

Nirjala Ekadashi

The significance of Ekadashi fasting was explained by Lord Krishna to Arjuna. There are twelve months in a year, and each month has two Ekadashis. Thus, there are twenty- four Ekadashis in a year.

The main purpose of fasting on these Ekadashis is to attain salvation and fulfill one's desires. Among all Ekadashis, Nirjala Ekadashi, Devashayani Ekadashi, and Divotsayani Ekadashi are considered the most important.

Nirjala Ekadashi fast is observed on the eleventh day of the bright half of the month of Jyeshtha without consuming water or food. It is believed that by observing this fast properly, one can obtain the benefits of all twenty-four Ekadashis.

It is said that once, Maharshi Vyasa visited the Pandavas. Bhima expressed his difficulty in observing Ekadashi fasts due to his excessive hunger. He requested a single fast that could provide the benefits of all Ekadashis. Maharshi Vyasa advised him to observe Nirjala Ekadashi in the month of Jyeshtha.

On Nirjala Ekadashi, you can drink water after performing Achaman (sipping water three times while chanting mantras), but you must refrain from eating and drinking for the rest of the day. By doing so, you will receive the blessings of twenty-four Ekadashis. Bhima followed this advice and therefore, this Ekadashi is also called called Bhimaseeni Ekadashi.

Another important Ekadashi is Devashayani Ekadashi, when Lord Vishnu goes to sleep for four months. This Ekadashi falls on the bright half of the month of Ashadha. Lord Vishnu should be put to sleep when the Sun enters the Cancer zodiac and awakened when the Sun enters the Libra zodiac. There is a story related to this Ekadashi.

In Satya Yuga, there was a king named Mandhata whose kingdom was prosperous and peaceful. Once, there was a drought in his kingdom that lasted for three years. The people suffered greatly due to this. King Mandhata was distressed and blamed himself for his people's suffering. He went to the forest and reached the ashram of Angera Rishi, the son of Brahma.

After welcoming the king, Angera Rishi asked the reason for his visit. The king said, "Due to three years of no rain, my people are suffering greatly." Angira Rishi replied, "There is a Shudra doing penance in your kingdom. If you kill him, the problem will be solved." The king said, "I cannot kill an innocent person. If there any other solution, please tell me.

The sage said, "O king, if you wish, observe Ekadashi on the bright half of the month of Ashadha and perform the puja properly. It will surely rain in your kingdom."

The king returned to his kingdom and, along with his ministers, observed the fast and performed the puja. As a result, it rained heavily, and his people were happy.

This fast is considered beneficial for both worldly pleasures and salvation in the afterlife. Lord Vishnu is pleased by this fast. The Chaturmas vrat (four-month fast) also begins on this day.

Somvar Vrat Katha

(Monday Fast Story)

The Monday fast is observed until the third part of the day. There are no strict rules regarding food and drink; one can eat only once a day and worship Lord Shiva with devotion.

Here is the story of Monday fast: There was a Sahukar (wealthy man) who had no children. He was deeply worried about this and devoted himself to Lord Shiva. Every Monday, he would go to the Shiva temple, light a lamp, observe the fast, and worship Lord Shiva.

Moved by his devotion, Parvati said to Shiva, "Lord, this is your true devotee. He worships you with such devotion every day. Grant him his wish." Shiva replied, "Dear, this world is a field of karma. You reap what you sow."

Parvati insisted, "If you do not grant his wish, why would people worship you?" Finally, Shiva blessed the devotee with a son, but he also said that the child would live only for twelve years.

The wealthy man continued to worship Shiva on Mondays. After some time, his wife became pregnant and gave birth to a beautiful son in the ninth month. The wealthy man received Shiva's blessing.

The father was neither very happy nor sad. When the son turned eleven, the father sent him to Kashi (Varanasi) to study. He called his brother-in-law, gave him a lot of money, and told him to accompany his nephew and spend money on yajnas (sacrifices) and feed Brahmins along the way.

On their way, the uncle and nephew reached a city where the king's daughter was about to get married to a one-eyed man. Seeing the uncle and nephew, the king was impressed and agreed to the marriage of his daughter with the nephew. After the wedding, the king gave the uncle a lot of money and sent him away.

While leaving, the nephew wrote on the daughter's chunri (dupatta), "Your marriage has happened with me. I am going to Kashi to study. The man you are leaving with is not your husband." The princess refused to leave and waited for her husband.

The nephew started studying in Kashi and continued to perform yajnas. When twelve years were completed, the nephew said he was feeling sleepy and wanted to rest inside while the yajna was going on. The uncle agreed and told him to go inside and sleep. As soon as the nephew entered, his lifespan ended. The uncle saw this but decided to wait until the yajna was completed.

When the yajna was over, everyone started crying. At that time, Shiva and Parvati were wandering in the mortal world. Hearing the cries, Parvati asked Shiva to give the boy another life as his father had served Shiva with great devotion. After Parvati's repeated requests, Shiva granted the boy another life, and he came back to life.

By then, the nephew's education was also complete. The uncle and nephew returned to the city where the nephew's wedding had taken place. The king recognized them and, giving them a lot of wealth, sent them away with his daughter.

The uncle brought his nephew's wife to his brother-in-law's city. When they reached home, they saw that his brother-in- law and sister-in-law were sitting sadly on the roof, saying that they would not come down until their son returned, otherwise they would jump off the roof and end their lives. Upon hearing their son's arrival, they were overjoyed and welcomed them with open arms.

Shiva fulfills the desires of those who worship him with devotion on Mondays.

Nag Panchami and Raksha Bandhan

A Brahmin lived happily with his family. He had a son and a daughter. His son was the apple of his parents' eye and possessed all virtues. One day, the Brahmin's wife suddenly fell ill and passed away. The Brahmin remarried, but his new wife couldn't love the children as much as their mother did, and the children led a very sad life. However, the father's love for his elder son was immense.

Wherever he went, he took his son with him and cared for both of them in every way. This did not please his stepmother at all. She was always trying to torment the children in one way or another. One day, the Brahmin went to the city to visit his employer. This was a good opportunity for the stepmother. She tricked the elder son and took him to the forest. In a secluded place near a river, she pushed the son into the water and returned home alone. When his sister asked where her brother was, the stepmother said that he had gone to the city with their father. The sister cried and wailed, and asked the people working in the forest where her brother went, and they explained that those who die become snakes.

The festival of Nag Panchami arrived. Every day, near the snake's burrow, the sister would say, "Snake brother, you are my brother." She would lament all the suffering that her stepmother had inflicted on her. The snake deity, hearing her sorrow, would understand her and send her away. Time passed, and the Raksha Bandhan festival arrived. All the brothers and sisters prepared to celebrate the festival. This sister, after completing all her household chores, went to the snake deity's burrow and said, "Tomorrow is Raksha Bandhan. I will come here tomorrow with a rakhi. You should appear in human form and accept the rakhi from me. Otherwise, I will cry until I die." Saying this, she returned home. All the snakes were worried. Until then, they had only taken lives. Now, someone was threatening to give up their life for them.

The troubled snakes approached Lord Vishnu, who was resting on the bed of Sheshnag. All night long, the snakes and snake deities prayed to Lord Vishnu. As their prayers intensified, the sister was also fasting and praying for her brother.

On that day, whatever food she got, she would save it for her brother. She thought in her mind, "After so many days, when I meet my brother, I will feed him many delicious dishes." All night, she stood on one leg and performed penance for her brother. At

3:30 AM, her penance was completed, and after taking a bath, she started doing household chores. After finishing her work, she took all kinds of dishes and went to the jungle, near the same snake's burrow, and started praying. Seeing her determination and amazing love for her brother, Lord Vishnu was pleased and gave her snake brother a human body. He was standing there, wearing beautiful clothes and a chariot, ready to get tied a rakhi on his wrist by his sister and give many gifts. The sister tied the rakhi on her brother's wrist, and the brother said to his sister, "We will live somewhere else and protect you in every way." Every sister, when she ties a rakhi on her brother's wrist, he vows to protect her always.

Raksha Bandhan

In India, every festival is deeply rooted in mythology, with each celebration connected to the gods, goddesses, and their timeless stories. Raksha Bandhan, a beloved festival primarily celebrated in North India, symbolizes the bond between brothers and sisters. It honors the tradition of sisters tying a protective thread, or rakhi, on their brothers' wrists, with the brothers pledging to protect their sisters in return. This festival, held on the full moon day of the Hindu month of Shravan (July-August), is steeped in various legends, each highlighting the deep bond between siblings.

One of the earliest stories linked to Raksha Bandhan involves Surya, the sun god, and his children, Yama and Yamuna. Yama, the god of death, and his brother Dharma received rakhi from their sister Yamuna. Deeply touched by her love and the protective gesture of tying a rakhi, Yama granted her the boon of immortality. This act of sibling devotion between Yamuna and Yama is believed to be one of the oldest examples of the protective and affectionate bond symbolized by Raksha Bandhan.

Another significant legend comes from the story of King Bali and the goddess Lakshmi. King Bali, a powerful devotee of Lord Vishnu, once asked Vishnu to protect his kingdom from enemies. Lord Vishnu, in his eternal devotion to his followers, agreed and left his heavenly abode to reside in Bali's kingdom. However, Vishnu's wife, the goddess Lakshmi, missed him deeply and wished for him to return home. Disguising herself as a Brahmin woman, Lakshmi visited King Bali's palace during Shravan Purnima. She tied a rakhi on Bali's wrist, revealing her true identity afterward and expressing her desire for Vishnu's return. Understanding her heartfelt wish, Bali requested Lord Vishnu to return home and bless his kingdom from afar, rather than living with him. From that day, Raksha Bandhan became a celebration not only of the bond between siblings but also of compassion and understanding.

Another famous tale associated with Raksha Bandhan comes from the Mahabharata. Lord Krishna, after killing the evil King Shishupala, was left with a bleeding wrist. Draupadi, the wife of the Pandavas, quickly tore a piece of her sari and tied it around Krishna's wrist to stop the bleeding. Moved by her kindness and the gesture of protection, Krishna promised Draupadi that he would always protect her in times of need. True to his word, he saved her honor during the infamous disrobing incident in the Kaurava court, fulfilling his vow of protection.

These stories, whether ancient or mythological, reflect the essence of Raksha Bandhan. The festival is not merely about the physical act of tying a rakhi but is a profound reminder of the unconditional love, duty, and lifelong promise of protection between brothers and sisters.

The Wrath of Shani Dev (Shani Devta Ka Prakop)

Once, Shani Dev (the god of Saturn) was standing at a crossroads. A Brahmin (a member of the highest Hindu caste) passed by and asked, "O God, what are you doing here?" Shani replied, "I am about to come here as the 'Sadhe Sati' (a challenging astrological bad period) upon the king of this place."

The Brahmin said, "O God, our king is very virtuous and protects everyone. Please do not do this to him." Shani Dev said, "I have decided that for at least two and a half moments or two and a half hours, I will definitely come upon someone." The Brahmin said, "Come upon us for two and a half hours. Let the king bear your wrath for just two and a half moments." (The Brahmin thought, "Two and a half hours will pass anyway in prayer and rituals.") Shani Dev agreed and became inattentive.

The Brahmin went to the riverbank and became engrossed in meditation and prayer. At that time, he saw two watermelons floating in the river. The Brahmin thought, "Let me cut and eat these watermelons first, then I will pray." As the Brahmin was cutting them, the king's procession arrived. The king's ministers told the king that these watermelons were the incarnations of the princes.

This Brahmin cut them into pieces. Now the princes, who had gone hunting, were no more. The king, overwhelmed with grief, rose and ordered that the Brahmin be hanged the next day. Preparations for the execution began. (This entire incident was the result of the half-moment of anger and the two-and-a-half-hour affliction of Saturn on the king.) The Brahmin pleaded, 'I am about to die anyway. Please grant me some time so that I can worship God.' The king agreed. The Brahmin began to meditate on God. Just then, the two princes returned from hunting. The king apologized to the Brahmin. By then, the two-and-a-half-hour affliction of Saturn on the Brahmin had ended. Hence, it is said that Saturn is a formidable deity who, even if present for a short time, will inevitably display his influence.

Hartalika Teej

This is a very difficult fast observed on the third day of the Shukla Paksha (bright fortnight) of the Bhadrapada month. Once, Shiva and Parvati were sitting on Mount Kailash. Parvati asked, "O Lord, if you are pleased with me, please tell me which fast, penance, charity, or virtuous deed can lead me to you." Shiva replied, "O Devi, there is one fast that surpasses all other fasts. I will tell you about it. Just as the moon is among the stars, the sun among the planets, the Brahmin among the castes, Vishnu among the deities, the Ganges among the rivers, the Mahabharata among the Puranas, the Samaveda among the Vedas, and the mind among the senses, this is the supreme fast. By observing this fast, you have attained half my seat."

Shiva then began the story, "In your previous life, you were born as Sati, the daughter of King Daksha and my wife. Due to certain events, you abandoned your body by jumping into the sacrificial fire at your father's house. In your next life, you were born as Parvati on Mount Himalaya. From childhood, you performed penance for me, standing in the scorching sun, eating dry leaves, getting soaked in the rain and standing in cold water in chilling weather.

You endured hardship, subjecting your body to various pains. Your father, Himalaya, was saddened by your situation and pondered over it.

At that time, the sage Narada came to your father and said, 'Lord Vishnu is very pleased and impressed by your daughter's penance and wants to marry her.' Hearing this, your father was overjoyed. What more could a father want than Vishnu himself as the groom for his daughter? Your father happily agreed, and Narada, filled with joy, departed for Vishnu's realm. Himalaya conveyed Narada's message to your mother, Maina. With a joyful heart, your mother informed you of your father's decision to marry you to Lord Vishnu. Upon hearing this, you were again determined to renounce your life.

When your dear friend heard about it, she counselled you against such foolishness and took you to a secluded cave in a dense forest, instructing you to perform penance there. On the third day, you created a Shiva lingam from sand and spent the entire night singing hymns, causing the throne of Lord Shiva on Mount Kailash to shake. I appeared before you. Pleased with your penance, I accepted you as my Ardhangini (other half) and returned to Kailash.

Meanwhile, your father was extremely worried that Lord Vishnu might arrive with his wedding party. He sent his relatives in all directions to search for you and himself proceeded towards that dense forest to search for you. They found you and accepted your penance. They brought you back home. In this way, your marriage with me took place, and you became my Ardhangini (other half)."

Every year on Teej, one should worship Lord Shiva in the morning, afternoon, and evening. Make a mandap with banana leaves and install a clay Shiva. Special worship is performed in the evening. After adorning Gauri, she is sent back to her father's house on the second day. Married women break their fast with light food. This fast is observed by young girls for a good husband and by married women for the longevity of their husbands. After the worship, offer a Suhag Pitari (auspicious items for married women) to a Brahmin woman and provide food and clothing to a Brahmin man.

It is believed that by observing this fast with discipline and restraint, Lord Shiva is pleased and grants desired results.

Shravan Monday

The month of Shravan, often accompanied by abundant rainfall, is regarded as a sacred period for worshiping Lord Shiva. This month holds special significance for Hindus, as it is believed that offering prayers to Lord Shiva during Shravan brings immense blessings. As stated in the *Shiva Purana,* "One should worship Shiva in Shravan." The spiritual energy of this time is so potent that the well-known Amarnath Yatra, a pilgrimage to Lord Shiva's holy shrine, takes place during this month. Devotees from various parts of India, such as Gangotri, Rishikesh, and Haridwar, carry holy water from the Ganges to perform the sacred ritual of pouring water on the Shiva lingam, an act of immense spiritual importance.

Lord Shiva, known as the "Mahadeva" or Great God, is considered the master of the three gunas (qualities) - *rajas* (passion), *sattva* (goodness), and *tamas* (ignorance). He maintains perfect balance over these qualities, which represent the forces that govern the universe. The offering of water to Lord Shiva during Shravan has deep symbolic roots, tied to an ancient event that occurred during the churning of the ocean (*Samudra Manthan*). The *Samudra Manthan* was a cosmic event where both gods and demons churned the ocean in search of *amrita* (the nectar of immortality). However, during the process, the deadly poison known as *Halahala* emerged, threatening to destroy all life. Lord Shiva, in his boundless compassion, drank the poison to save the universe. Though the poison did not harm him, it caused his throat to turn blue, earning him the title of "Neelkanth," or the one with the blue throat. To ease the burning sensation from the poison, the gods poured water on him. Since that time, devotees continue to offer water and milk to the Shiva lingam, especially during Shivaratri, believing that this ritual brings peace and prosperity.

While offering water to Lord Shiva, devotees chant the powerful mantra "Om Namah Shivaya" and offer bel leaves, inscribed with the sacred name "Ram-Ram." According to the *Shiva Purana,* offering different substances during the *abhisheka* (a ritual pouring of liquids over the deity) yields various benefits:

- **Juice of sugarcane**: Bestows wealth.
- **Honey**: Invokes the blessings of Goddess Lakshmi.
- **Milk**: Brings the joy of having a son.

- **Ganges water**: Grants peace of mind.

In addition to these rituals, an important historical event unfolded during Shravan. According to legend, Sati, the daughter of Daksha Prajapati, went uninvited to her father's home and witnessed her husband, Shiva, being insulted. Unable to bear the humiliation, she jumped into the sacrificial fire, wishing to be reborn as Shiva's wife. In her next life, Sati was reborn as Parvati, the daughter of the Himalayas. She performed intense penance and observed a fast starting on the first Monday of Shravan until Lord Shiva was pleased and accepted her as his wife.

Today, unmarried women follow in Parvati's footsteps by fasting on the Mondays of Shravan, praying for a good husband. Married women also observe the fast to pray for the long life and well-being of their husbands. Thus, the month of Shravan holds immense spiritual significance for both men and women, as devotees seek blessings, peace, and prosperity from Lord Shiva.

For the Son - Har Chhath

The festival of Har Chhath is celebrated by a boy's mother on the sixth (Chhath) day in the month of Bhadon (two days before Janmashtami) for her son's well-being. There are two stories associated with it, which are told and heard among people after the puja.

First Story

Once upon a time, there lived a mother-in-law and her daughter-in-law in a prosperous household, blessed with cows and buffaloes. Among them, the mother-in-law had a special affection for one buffalo, whom she lovingly named "Anna Bhainsia." This buffalo was not just a source of milk; it was a cherished member of the family. The mother-in-law took exceptional care of Anna Bhainsia, personally bathing her, keeping her enclosure clean, and milking her regularly. The bond they shared was evident, and Anna Bhainsia thrived under her loving attention.

One day, the mother-in-law had to leave for her parents' home due to some urgent work. Before departing, she earnestly instructed her daughter-in-law to take special care of Anna Bhainsia and the other animals. However, once the mother-in-law left, the daughter-in-law's true colors began to show. She neglected all the cows and buffaloes, but her treatment of Anna Bhainsia was particularly harsh. Instead of providing the care that the animals deserved, she carelessly threw household garbage into their enclosure and failed to clean or bathe them. Poor Anna Bhainsia became increasingly sad and distressed under this mistreatment.

Realizing that her situation had become unbearable, Anna Bhainsia decided to leave the home that once felt safe and nurturing. One day, taking advantage of the moment, she wandered off into the nearby forest, seeking solace and peace away from the harsh environment.

When the mother-in-law returned home, she immediately noticed the absence of Anna Bhainsia and felt a pang of worry. Concerned, she asked her daughter-in-law about the beloved buffalo, but to her dismay, the daughter-in-law remained silent, offering no explanation. Sensing something was wrong, the mother-in-law's heart sank, and she set off toward the forest, driven by her love for Anna Bhainsia.

As she reached the forest, she found Anna Bhainsia crying, looking lost and forlorn. The sight broke the mother-in-law's heart, and she approached the buffalo with gentle words of comfort. "My dear Anna Bhainsia," she pleaded, "how can we celebrate the Har Chhath puja without you? You are so important to us." The mother-in-law poured her love and affection into her words, coaxing Anna Bhainsia to return home with her.

Eventually, the mother-in-law's sincere efforts paid off, and Anna Bhainsia, touched by the warmth of her affection, agreed to return. This beautiful bond between the mother-in-law and her buffalo not only brought joy back into their lives but also reinforced the significance of cow's milk, curd, and cream during the Har Chhath festival, symbolizing love, care, and gratitude in the family.

Second Story

Women gather together near a pond to perform the Har Chhath puja. The story goes like this: There was a kingdom facing a severe water shortage. They dug many ponds, but water still didn't come. The king and his people performed various prayers and rituals, but to no avail. One day, a wise man came to the king's court and offered a solution, but it was very difficult, especially for the king. When asked, the wise man said that if the king sacrificed his son, the kingdom would receive water. The king was deeply saddened but decided to sacrifice his son for the welfare of his kingdom.

He told his queen to go to her parents' place for some time while he took care of their son. The queen left, and the king sacrificed his son. As soon as the sacrifice was completed, water started flowing throughout the kingdom. The queen made preparations to return to her kingdom during the time of Har Chhath.

The queen also came to know that water had started flowing in her kingdom. While she was still on her way, she saw her son eating mahua (a type of flower) near a pond. She became very angry with the king for leaving their son alone. She brought her son back to the palace and questioned the king about his son's whereabouts. The grief-stricken king couldn't speak, tears streaming down his face. After much insistence from the queen, the king revealed the truth.

The queen then showed her son to the king and told him how she found him. It is said that Har Chhath Devi was pleased with the king's sacrifice for his people and returned his son to him. From then on, everyone in the kingdom lived happily and peacefully, and Har Chhath Devi blessed them all.

The Story of Annakuta and Govardhan

During the Dwapar Yuga, young Krishna, with innocent curiosity, approached Nanda Baba one day and asked, "Baba, what is the reason for today's celebration? I see everyone preparing so many dishes in their homes." Smiling at Krishna's childlike wonder, Nanda Baba explained, "Today, we worship Indra Devata, the god of rain, and these dishes are made as offerings to honor him."

Krishna, full of questions, asked, "Who is Indra Devata? What does he do? Why do we need to worship him?" His innocent curiosity led Nanda Baba to elaborate further. "Once, there was a severe drought in our region due to a lack of rain. The crops withered, and people were desperate. The Brahmins advised that we should worship Indra Devata, who governs the rain, as well as the Govardhan mountain, to bring relief. The people of Vrindavan followed their advice, and soon after, heavy rains came, reviving the crops and bringing prosperity. Since that time, we honor Indra Devata each year by preparing special dishes and offering prayers."

Krishna, reflecting on this tradition, responded thoughtfully, "But what would happen if people did not worship Indra Devata or the Govardhan mountain? What if they chose not to follow this practice?" His question sparked curiosity among the people of Vrindavan, who were captivated by Krishna's words. He suggested that they skip the worship and observe the consequences, proposing that perhaps Govardhan mountain itself should be honored instead.

Agreeing with Krishna's suggestion, the people of Vrindavan decided not to prepare the feast for Indra Devata that year. When Indra Devata noticed this, he was enraged by what he saw as a slight to his honor. In his fury, he declared, "Let it rain so much that the entire Braj region is submerged under water!" Dark clouds gathered, and a torrential downpour began. The rain was relentless, threatening to flood the whole region and destroy everything in its path.

At this moment, Lord Krishna revealed his divine nature. To protect the people of Vrindavan and their cattle, Krishna lifted the mighty Govardhan mountain with the little finger of his left hand, using it as an umbrella to shelter them from the storm. For seven days and nights, the rains lashed down, but Krishna held the mountain aloft effortlessly, shielding the people and their cows. Indra's pride was defeated, and he realized the greatness of Krishna. Humbled, Indra ceased the storm.

From that day forward, the people of Vrindavan no longer saw Govardhan as just a mountain; they revered it as a form of Krishna himself. They began to worship Govardhan annually, honoring the mountain and remembering the protection Krishna had bestowed upon them. This event not only glorified the Govardhan mountain but also marked the triumph of humility over pride and the power of devotion over arrogance.

Krishna Janmashtami

In the Dwapar Yuga, the earth, oppressed by the atrocities of demons, took the form of a cow and ascended to heaven, reaching Brahma. She narrated her suffering to Brahma, who, upon hearing her plight, went to Lord Vishnu with all the deities. Upon hearing their pleas, Lord Vishnu declared, "All of you deities should descend to earth and take human form, while I will be born from Devaki's womb." With this blessing, all the deities descended to Braj, taking the forms of Nanda, Yashoda, Gopas, and Gopikas. The story of Krishna's birth is as follows:

In Mathura, there lived a kind-hearted king named Ugrasen, who cared deeply for his people. His wife was Dramila. They had two children: Prince Kansa and Princess Devaki. Both siblings loved each other dearly and grew up together. While Ugrasen was a benevolent and compassionate king, Kansa was a cruel and ruthless ruler.

As time passed, Devaki reached marriageable age. She was married to Vasudev, a dear friend of Kansa. Overflowing with love for his sister, Kansa pulled her chariot from the wedding mandap, leading her away.

Then an ominous event occurred. A voice from the sky announced, "Kansa, the very person who is so lovingly sending off his sister today, will be killed by her eighth child." Disturbed by this, Kansa immediately prepared to kill Devaki. Vasudev pleaded with Kansa, promising to give him all their children. Kansa agreed and released Devaki but imprisoned both of them. Strict guards were placed to ensure that any newborn child would be killed immediately. Devaki and Vasudev's children were consistently met with such a fate.

When Devaki was about to give birth to her seventh child, it was night. They tried to save the child and succeeded. The guards were asleep. Vasudev quietly went to Gokul, where his other wife Rohini lived, and left the child with her. The child was later named Balarama. The news of the child's stillbirth reached Kansa, who was relieved.

Now, the eighth child was about to be born. Kansa tightened security and bound Devaki and Vasudev with chains. In the month of Sawan, on the eighth day of the dark fortnight, Lord Krishna was born in the prison. It was a dark, stormy night with thunder and lightning. Suddenly, the chained couple's hands and feet became untied, the prison doors opened, and all the guards were asleep. Vasudev decided to leave the child across the Yamuna River to Nanda's house, who was his friend. He placed

Krishna in a basket and set off for Gokul. The Yamuna River was flowing at its fullest, and it seemed as though the river was trying to touch Krishna's feet. As soon as the river touched his feet, it calmed down. When Vasudev reached Nandgaon, he found out that in his friend Nand's house, Yashoda had given birth to a daughter on the same day. While Yashoda was asleep, Vasudev carefully placed Krishna in her arms and took the girl back to the prison. As soon as he returned to the prison, the doors closed, and their hands and feet were bound again. The baby's cries woke up the guards, who rushed to inform Kansa of the birth of a daughter. Vasudev thought that Kansa might spare the girl's life upo n hearing the news.

However, when Kansa arrived, he became enraged and was about to throw the baby on the ground when the baby uttered, "The one who will kill you is in Gokul." With these words, the baby vanished. Kansa then sent Putana, a demoness, to kill Krishna through a malevolent plan. He also employed other means to harm Krishna, but all his attempts were unsuccessful. Krishna, with his mischievous and playful antics, captivated everyone.

As Krishna entered his teenage years, he had many friends, including cowherd boys and Gopikas. Under the loving care of Yashoda and Nanda, he spent his days joyfully. He engaged in various activities.

Krishna had a special affection for Radha, the daughter of Vrishbhanu. During the moonlit nights, when the raaslila (a dance and song performance) used to take place, Krishna would often challenge the venomous Kaliya serpent and fight with him while playing with the ball along with his friends.

Kansa, ever determined to kill Krishna, constantly devised plans. He eventually summoned Krishna and Balarama to his capital, Mathura, with the intention of killing them. The news of this caused great sadness among the Gopas, Gopikas, Yashoda, and Nanda. Despite their pleas, Krishna and Balarama departed for Mathura.

Kansa made numerous attempts to kill Krishna, including crushing him under a mad elephant and challenging him to a wrestling match. However, Krishna emerged victorious in every encounter. Finally, with his Sudarshan Chakra (discus), Krishna killed Kansa, who was terrified of his own evil deeds.

One remarkable aspect of Janmashtami is its enduring popularity. Even after thousands of years, people continue to celebrate this festival with great enthusiasm. Just as the birth of a new-born is celebrated, so too is Krishna's 'Chhathi' (the festival on sixth day after birth) is celebrated with great fervour. Various offerings, including different types of food, are prepared. Processions and tableaux depicting Krishna's many forms are also organized.

Mathura and Vrindavan continue to be deeply influenced by Krishna. The joyful atmosphere and festive spirit of Janmashtami are evident in the people's celebrations. The "Holi" of flowers' is a particular attraction in these regions.

Dussehra & Durga Pooja

Dussehra is celebrated on the tenth day of the bright half of Ashwin month (October). It is also known as Dasara, Dashara, Dashayan, Navratri, and Durgothsav. The word "Dussehra" means "ten days" (dasha meaning ten and aaha meaning day). Dussehra holds a special place among Hindu festivals. For centuries, people have been celebrating this festival for nine days in various ways to please God.

In some places, women and girls can be seen dancing Garba in Gujarat, while in others, Ramlila plays are performed for nine days, culminating with the burning of Ravana. The Puranas describe four yugas: Satyuga, Treta, Dwapar, and Kaliyuga. Each yuga lasts for thousands of years. During the Treta Yuga, King Dasharatha ruled in Ayodhya. He had four sons: Rama, Lakshmana, Bharata, and Shatrughna. He had three wives: Kaushalya, Kaikeyi, and Sumitra.

Rama was the eldest son, so Dasharatha wanted to give him the kingdom. This did not please his third wife, Kaikeyi. She reminded King Dasharatha about the two boons he had promised to give toKaikeyi. Dasharatha told her to ask two boons.

One of the two boons that King Dasharatha granted was to his son Bharata, who was the heir to the throne. The other boon was for Ramchandraji, who was exiled to the forest for fourteen years. Even though Dasharatha had made a promise, he was deeply saddened by this decision and eventually died of grief.

When Rama was about to leave for the forest, his wife Sita and brother Lakshmana decided to accompany him. Bharata and Shatrughna were not in Ayodhya at the time; they were visitingtheir maternal grandmother. In the forest, the demoness Surpanakha, who was the sister of Ravana, fell in love with Lakshmana and tried to seduce him. When Lakshmana rejected her advances, she became angry and persisted with her advances. Ultimately he became very angry and mutilated her nose.

Surpanakha went to Ravana's court and complained about the insult she had suffered. Ravana, enraged by his sister's condition, disguised himself as a sage and abducted Sita. At that time, Rama and Lakshmana were hunting for the demon Maricha. When they returned to their hut and found Sita missing, they were devastated.

Ravana carried Sita away to Lanka, where he imprisoned her in the Ashok Vatika. The demonesses guarded the garden, and

Ravana would visit Sita daily, pleading with her to look at him once. Sita consistently refused his requests.

Meanwhile, Rama, when he reached 'Parn Kuti', did not find Sita. Heartbroken by Sita's disappearance, wandered through the forest in search of her. He eventually encountered the wise monkey Hanuman, who reassured him and promised to definitely find Sita. And on the way, he also encountered Jatayu, a vulture who was mortally wounded. Jatayu informed him of the direction Ravana had taken Sita.

Hanuman leaped across the ocean and reached Lanka during the day, but he waited until night to enter. He found that all the demons were asleep during the day, but they became active at night. Hanuman deduced that this was Lanka, the city of Ravana.

He explored the city and found it to be filled with immense wealth and grandeur. He then discovered the palace of Vibhishana, Ravana's brother, which was simple and unadorned. The palace had a tulsi plant and the name "Rama" written on it. Hanuman concluded that this must be the abode of a saint and entered. He inquired about Sita's whereabouts and was informed that she was in the Ashok Vatika. Hanuman went there and introduced himself to Sita, showing her Rama's ring as proof of his identity. Sita was reassured by this.

Hanuman promised Sita that Rama would soon arrive to rescue her. He then returned to Rama, where Sugriva, Jamvant, and other monkey warriors were waiting. Upon hearing the news of Sita's location, they prepared to attack Lanka. A fierce battle ensued between Rama and Ravana, which lasted for ten days. On the tenth day of Dussehra, Ravana was finally defeated and killed. Hence, the festival is named Dussehra, meaning "ten days".

In some places, people celebrate Dussehra by establishing a kalash (pot) for nine days and reciting the Ramayana daily, followed by a havan (fire sacrifice). It is said that havan eliminates evils like anger, greed, lust, pride, attachment, selfishness, arrogance, injustice, inhumanity, and ego, which are represented by Ravana's ten heads.

There are other stories associated with Dussehra as well.

One such story is about a Brahmin named Devadatta and his son, Kautsa. Kautsa was a very intelligent and promising child. He received education from the sage Varatantu and learned various arts. When it was time for Kautsa to leave his teacher, he wanted to give him a dakshina (gift). The sage initially refused but eventually agreed to accept 140 gold coins. However, Devadatta didn't have that much money.

He went to King Raghu, who was known for his generosity, and requested help. Even King Raghu didn't have enough gold, so he appealed to Kubera, the god of wealth, to rain gold coins from the Apti and Shanu trees. Kubera granted his wish, and Kautsa was able to give the sage his desired dakshina and distribute the remaining gold to the poor.

Even today, some people give the leaves of the Apti tree tree (wish-fulfilling tree) to their youngers as a token of wealth.

Another story is related to the goddess Durga and the demon Mahishasura. Mahishasura was a powerful demon who troubled all three worlds. He frightened and troubled even the Devtas with his might.

When the demon Mahishasura terrorized the three worlds, the gods sought refuge with Brahma, Vishnu, and Mahesh. They united their powers to create the goddess Shakti, also known as Durga. All the gods contributed their powers to help Durga defeat Mahishasura.

Durga descended to Earth and engaged in a fierce battle with Mahishasura for nine days. Finally, on the tenth day, she vanquished the demon with her trident. This victory is still celebrated today as Durga Puja.

Durga Puja is marked with great enthusiasm, especially in Bengal. People wear new clothes every day, and elaborate pandals (temporary structures) are erected to house the idols of Durga, Saraswati, Lakshmi, Kartikeya, and Ganesha. Sometimes, the idols of Jaya and Vijaya, Durga's companions, are also placed in the pandals.

People visit the pandals with devotion, offering prayers and enjoying cultural programs like dance and music. Numerous food stalls are set up to cater to the visitors. On the ninth day, a grand puja is performed, and on the tenth day, the idols are immersed in a river or pond. People accompany the idols with singing and dancing, marking the end of the nine-day celebration.

Bhai Jiyutia

In Odisha, people observe a fast on the seventh day of the festival, known as Saptami. They refrain from eating after midnight and break their fast on the eighth day, Ashtami. A puja is held in the pandals at night, and people bring rice from the pandals to their homes.

On the ninth day, sisters make mounds of sand near ponds or rivers. One mound for each brother is made. They place seven neem sticks in each mound and offer prayers with offerings like amla leaves, rice, chickpeas, and whole moong dal. They then place the offerings in a leaf container with curd and rice and three grains of whole moong. The leaf container is put in an earthen diya (lamp). The contents are eaten while standing on the riverbank. They ask each other as what is being eaten. The reply given is that Durga ji's Prasad is being eaten. They don't chew the food but swallow it whole.

Upon returning home, sisters apply roli and sandalwood paste to their brothers' foreheads and perform aarti. They offer their brothers suitable gifts and then eat the prasad themselves after feeding their brothers. Brothers also reciprocate by giving gifts to their sisters. Regardless of their age, siblings celebrate this festival with great devotion. This is a unique way to celebrate Dussehra in Odisha.

Sharad Purnima

Sharad Purnima is a festival celebrated on the full moon night of Ashwin month (October). Nature becomes clean and white after the rainy season. The heat of summer is relieved. Preparations are made for the arrival of autumn. It is believed that on this day, the moon is closest to the earth and showers nectar on the earth with its bright rays.

Lakshmi ji was born on this day. This festival is especially celebrated in South Bengal, Odisha, Uttar Pradesh, and Madhya Pradesh. The most important aspect of this festival is celebrating it at night. All other Hindu festivals are celebrated during the day or morning. In Odisha, this festival is called Kumar Purnima.

They believe that Kartikeya, the son of Gauri Shankar, was born on this day. Unmarried girls get up early in the morning, offer water to the sun, fast for the whole day, make kheer, offer it to the moon, and take prasad at midnight.

There is also a scientific reason behind eating kheer on Sharad Purnima. During this time, the days are hot and the nights are cold. This can lead to an increase in bile in the body. It is believed that eating kheer can help alleviate bile-related stomach problems.

Mathura, Vrindavan, and Nathdwara hold special significance for this festival. In Vrindavan, Lord Krishna performed the Rasa Lila dance with Radha and the gopis on this day. Krishna is said to have created 32 ragas and 54 raginis using his flute.

There are also stories associated with this day. It is said that on this day, Kamadeva, the god of love, was returning victorious from conquering the three worlds. On the way, he met Narad muni. Narad muni told him that in Braj there is a boy called Krishna. Fight him and win, then your braveness will be established,

Upon hearing about the young boy Krishna in Vrindavan, Kamadeva challenged him on Sharad Poornima day to a duel. Krishna emerged victorious and let Kamadeva go, predicting that he would be born as his son, Pradyumna, in his next life.

Another popular story involves two sisters who were observing the Sharad Purnima fast. The elder sister performed the fast with devotion, and her children thrived. The younger sister, however, performed the fast only superficially. As a result, all her children died. Grieving, she went to the sage Shandilya for guidance. He advised her to perform the fast with sincerity and devotion.

The younger sister continued to keep fast for many years but her new born children would not survive. On Poornima day again a child was born to her but he was dead. She wrapped the dead child in a white cloth and laid it on a cradle. When the elder sister visited, the younger sister asked her to sit on the cradle. As soon as the elder sister touched the cradle, the child started crying. The elder sister was surprised and said that if she had sat on the cradle, the child would have died. The younger sister, still crying, explained that the child had already died but was revived by the elder sister's virtuous fast. From then on, both sisters observed the Sharad Purnima fast with devotion and were blessed with prosperity.

Karwa Chauth

Karwa Chauth is a festival celebrated on the fourth day of the dark half of Kartik month (October). After the summer heat, the weather starts to cool down. Nature's joy and influence can be seen everywhere.

On this day, newly married women wake up early in the morning to prepare sargi, a pre-dawn meal. The mother-in-law prepares sargi for her daughter-in-law as a sign of love and affection. The women then start their fast without drinking water or eating food. They spend the day getting ready or doing other activities like watching movies.

There are several stories associated with Karwa Chauth. One story is about a wealthy man who lived with his wife, seven sons, their wives, and a daughter. When the daughter was ready to get married, she found a suitable husband. The daughter was very close to her brothers, and when Karwa Chauth came, the mother-in-law and all the daughters-in-law observed the fast, the daughter who was her mother also observed Karwa Chauth fast.

At dinner time, when the mother was serving food, she announced that the daughter would not eat as she was fasting for Karwa Chauth. Seeing the worried expressions of her brothers, the mother revealed that the daughter could only eat after offering arghya to the moon.

The youngest brother, who was very playful, suggested a plan. He said that they should light a fire behind the trees and one of the brothers should stand in front of it, holding a sieve. When the sister sees the fire, she will think it's the moon and offer arghya, allowing everyone else to eat. The brothers followed the plan, and when the sister was about to offer arghya, the brothers asked her if the moon had risen. The sister thought that there may be different moon for different persons. As such she replied to her sisters-in-law that their moon had not risen yet, but hers had risen.

The sister offered arghya to the fake moon and returned to eat, unaware that she had been tricked. However, as soon as she finished eating, she received a message that her husband's condition had worsened. Upon hearing this, she became anxious and rushed to her husband's house. Her mother advised her to seek blessings from respected people on her way. The sister met many revered individuals and sought their blessings, but she didn't receive any blessings.

When she reached her husband's house, she found his condition to be very critical. The doctors had given up hope, and the astrologer warned her about the consequences of offering arghya to the fake moon.

The daughter received this punishment for breaking the Karwa Chauth fast. As a remedy, she was advised to fast for a year on every Chauth and pray to Lord Ganesha. She was also told that he would recover if she served her husband wholeheartedly with body and mind. She followed this advice and served her husband diligently until the next Karwa Chauth.

On the next Karva Chauth, happy with the devotion of the daughter, the goddess of Karwa Chauth arrived beautifully adorned. After much persuasion, she agreed to exchange Karvas with her daughter and said these words. From then on, the tradition of exchanging Karvas began.

"The sister of seven brothers should take Karva. She who cannot remain hungry should take Karva. She who cannot remain thirsty should take Karva.

She who sees the moon in a dream should take Karva."

Saying this, the Chauth mother was about to leave. She did not give the blessing of a husband to the married woman. When the sister pleaded, she said that her ten sisters would come, and then she should ask them for the blessing of remaining a married woman. Nine goddesses came and also exchanged Karvas, but they did not bless her to remain a married woman forever. When the ninth Chauth mother was about to leave, the sister became very sad. Holding her feet, she said, "Mother, if you are pleased with the service I have done to my husband, please give me a blessing."

The Chauth goddess said, "My sister will come now. She is ugly but has a gentle heart. Pray to her, and your prayer will surely turn into a blessing." When the Chauth mother arrived, she exchanged karva ten times.

The goddess blessed her and said, "May you always be blessed with a happy married life." The daughter was overjoyed and became a symbol of marital bliss and longevity.

There are other short stories related to Karwa Chauth.

One story is about a Brahmin couple. The Brahmin would leave for work, and his wife would cook delicious food and eat it alone, pretending to be hungry when her husband returned. The kind- hearted Brahmin believed her and supported her.

One year, their neighbours revealed the truth to the Brahmin. On the next Karwa Chauth, The Brahmin left from the front door and surreptitiously came inside from the back door. The Brahmin followed his wife and observed her behaviour. He saw her eating heartily and pretending to be hungry. The Brahmin's heart was broken, He confronted his wife and told her to undertake the fast only if she feels like it and there is no need to show off. His wife realised her folly and asked for forgiveness. Brahmin was kind hearted and forgave her. His wife decided to continue to observe Karwa Chauth with sincerity.

Another story mentions that Parvati once asked Lord Shiva about the secret to a happy married life. Shiva revealed that observing Karwa Chauth with devotion was the key to attaining eternal marital bliss.

In ancient times, there was a very old washerman living near the village of Tung Bhadra with his wife, Karwa. The husband was very old and frail. The wife would wash clothes while the husband sat there. One day, a crocodile emerged from a pond and tried to drag the husband away. The helpless husband cried out for help, and Karwa rushed to the rescue.

When Karwa reached the gates of the Yamlok, she demanded that Yama, the god of death, punish the crocodile for trying to harm her husband. Yama replied that the crocodile still had some time to live and could not be punished.

Karwa, who was a devoted wife, threatened to curse Yama if he did not save her husband. Fearing the curse, Yama sent the crocodile to hell and blessed Karwa with eternal marital bliss. This incident occurred on Karwa Chauth. Karwa Chauth is a significant festival for married women, who observe it with devotion for a happy and long-lasting marriage.

Devashthani Ekadashi

Devshthani Ekadashi, often referred to as the "Diwali of the gods," is a significant Hindu festival that marks the symbolic marriage of Tulsi, the sacred basil plant, and Lord Vishnu in the form of Saligram. This day holds deep spiritual meaning and is celebrated with great devotion.

According to ancient legend, Vrinda, the virtuous daughter of a sage, was cursed and transformed into the lifeless Tulsi plant. Despite this transformation, Vrinda continued her intense penance and unwavering devotion to Lord Vishnu, praying for reunification with him. Pleased by her devotion, Lord Vishnu appeared in the form of Saligram, a sacred black stone, to marry her. As a mark of his blessing, he declared that even a single leaf from the Tulsi plant would have the power to turn any offering into nectar, thus granting Tulsi an exalted position in Hindu rituals. Since then, Tulsi leaves have become an integral part of worship and are used in religious offerings.

Devshthani Ekadashi also marks the day when the gods awaken after a four-month period of divine slumber, known as Chaturmas. During these months, auspicious ceremonies such as marriages and other sacred rites are paused. With the arrival of Devshthani Ekadashi, these activities resume, signifying a fresh beginning of spiritual endeavors and festive celebrations.

Among the 24 Ekadashis observed throughout the year, Devshthani Ekadashi holds a special place. It is believed that fasting on this day and performing the accompanying rituals with sincere devotion can lead to moksha, or salvation. Observing this fast is considered highly meritorious, and it is said to offer rewards far greater than even the most elaborate Vedic rituals, such as the Rajasuya Yagya or Ashvamedha Yagna.

An interesting story highlights the importance of this Ekadashi. A wealthy man named Ghanshyam Das once visited the Hanuman Garhi temple and bathed in the sacred Sarayu River. There, he heard a sage named Mohan Das Baba explaining the immense spiritual benefits of observing Ekadashi. The sage told the gathered crowd that fasting on Ekadashi could bestow greater blessings than performing grand sacrifices. Intrigued, Ghanshyam Das asked why, despite the great rewards, more people did not observe the Ekadashi fast. Mohan Das Baba admitted that even he found it difficult to endure the physical hardships of fasting and confessed that the practice was more commonly observed in the Jagannath Puri temple.

Hearing this, the crowd dispersed, leaving Mohan Das Baba filled with remorse for his words. Realizing the gravity of his statement, he apologized to Ghanshyam Das and vowed to not only observe the fast himself but also to spread awareness of its significance.

It is said that observing Ekadashi with sincere devotion, chanting the holy names of Lord Krishna, and performing good deeds can lead one to spiritual liberation. Devotees are encouraged to spend the day immersed in pure thoughts, religious activities, and acts of kindness, as this day offers a unique opportunity for spiritual upliftment.

Dhanteras

Dhanteras is the first festival of the five-day Diwali celebration, which occurs in the Ashwin month (October). It is also known as Dhan Triyodashi or Dhanvantri Triyodashi. Dhanteras is celebrated on the thirteenth day of the dark half of the month, with the hope of receiving wealth and prosperity. Hence, it is also called Dhanteras.

From this day onwards, shops are adorned with various gifts and decorations. People light up their homes with colorful lights and rangoli. They also light lamps and exchange gifts with each other while wishing good luck. It is considered auspicious to buy utensils, silver, and gold items on this day. Some people also enjoy gambling or playing cards on Dhanteras.

There are two popular stories associated with Dhanteras that families often share with each other.

Once, Yama asked his messengers if they had ever faced any difficulties or failures while carrying out their duty of taking souls. The terrified messengers replied that they never experienced any fear or failure, as they were simply following Yama's orders.

Yama then asked them to share any instances where they had hesitated or felt pity while taking a soul. The messengers hesitated and finally admitted to an incident.

A 16-year-old prince was scheduled to die on the fourth day of his marriage. His horoscope also predicted this. The prince's newlywed wife found out about this and decided to save her husband. The prince was destined to die by snake bite while sleeping.

She filled her room with lights, music, and valuable items to distract the angel of death. She kept her husband awake all night with her singing and playing instruments. When the angel of death arrived, the bright lights and music blinded him, and he was so captivated by the sounds that he stayed to listen.

As a result, the prince survived the fateful hour, and his untimely death was averted due to his wife's cleverness and devotion. Since then on Dhanteras, people decorate their homes with lights and buy utensils according to their means.

There's a story associated with this festival: Once, Lord Vishnu and Lakshmi came to Earth. Vishnu told Lakshmi to wait while he went in a certain direction. Lakshmi thought there must be something important and followed him.

On their way, Lakshmi saw mustard fields and adorned herself with their yellow flowers. She also saw sugarcane fields and ate some sugarcane. When Vishnu returned, he was angry and told Lakshmi that she would have to serve a farmer for twelve years as punishment.

Lakshmi agreed, as she could not disobey Vishnu's orders. She served the farmer and his wife diligently for twelve years. The farmer's house prospered due to Lakshmi's presence. At the end of the twelve years, when Lakshmi was about to leave, the farmer and his wife begged her to stay.

Vishnu appeared to take Lakshmi away. Before leaving, Vishnu gave the couple four coins and told them to go for a bath in the Ganges and return and that they will wait for the farmer and his wife. On their way to the Ganges, the couple lost the coins. The goddess Ganga appeared and told them that the couple they had left behind were none other than Vishnu and Lakshmi. Upon hearing this they ran back and fell on the feet of Vishnu and Lakshmi.

The farmer insisted that they should not leave him and his wife alone.Vishnu replied, "Lakshmi has already completed her punishment. She is not meant to stay in one place for long." Despite the farmer's pleas, Vishnu and Lakshmi departed.

Before leaving, Vishnu and Lakshmi blessed the farmer and his wife, saying, "Today is Dhanteras. Clean your house, light lamps, and offer prayers. I will visit you in an invisible form, and my blessings will always be with you." With these words, Vishnu and Lakshmi disappeared, spreading light everywhere. May Vishnu and Lakshmi bless every one like they have blessed the farmer and his wife.

This story highlights the importance of observing Dhanteras and seeking blessings from Lord Vishnu and Lakshmi.

Naraka Chaturdashi

Naraka Chaturdashi is the second day of the five-day festival of Diwali, which falls on the fourteenth day of the dark fortnight of the month of Kartik. It is also known as Choti Diwali. On this day, people engaged in Diwali preparations clean their homes and light lamps in all the drains and places where dirt accumulates. Some people also light fourteen lamps in every room of their house.

A story related to this festival is given below.

There was once a king named Narakasura in the kingdom of Pragjyotishapur, located in the southern part of Nepal. He was a cruel and inhuman ruler. He defeated Indra Dev in heaven and took away Aditi's ear rings. Aditi was not only the guardian of the celestial realm but also a relative of Satyabhama, Krishna's wife. Narakasura had imprisoned 16,000 girls, including daughters of sages and celestial maidens.

When Satyabhama heard about this, she went to Krishna and asked for strength to kill Narakasura. Narakasura had a boon that he could only be killed by a woman. Satyabhama, riding a chariot driven by Krishna himself, set out to vanquish Narakasura. Narakasura was defeated and killed on the night of Triyodashi. All the imprisoned girls were liberated, and Aditi's ear rings were returned. To save the girls from self-blame, Krishna accepted them all as his wives.

After Narakasura's death, Krishna applied his blood to his forehead as a sign of victory and returned to his palace with the sixteen thousand girls. In the palace, the dasis bathed and purified the girls with ubtan (a paste made of gram flour, herbs and spices). Narakasura was so cruel that after his death, his mother, Bhudevi, requested that this day not be mourned but celebrated as a festival.

Even today, in some parts of Maharashtra, people apply a kumkum tilak made from sour fruit, symbolizing Narakasura's blood. They also break a gourd, representing Narakasura's head. On Naraka Chaturdashi, there is a tradition of taking an oil bath early in the morning and lighting lamps and fireworks in the evening.

Another story associated with this festival is about King Bali, who ruled the underworld. His ambitions were causing great trouble to all the gods.

All the gods prayed to Lord Vishnu for help. Lord Vishnu, disguised as a dwarf Brahmin, went to Bali and asked for land to build a house. Bali agreed to give him as much land as he could cover in three steps. Vishnu, in his true form, took one step and covered the entire heaven, the second step covered the underworld (Pataal Lok), and then asked Bali where to place the third step. Bali, realizing his mistake, offered his head as the place for the third step. As soon as Vishnu put his leg on Bali’s head, Bali got into Patal Lok.

Vishnu was pleased with Bali's generosity and blessed him to visit the earth every year on Naraka Chaturdashi and light lamps are lit in people's homes.

Diwali

First Story

There was once a potter who had seven sons. All seven sons worked during the day and returned home in the evening to cook and sleep. The eldest son got married, and when his wife came to the house, she was surprised to see seven hearths. She broke six hearths and cooked a delicious meal on the remaining hearth. When the seven sons returned home from work, they saw the broken hearths and asked their sister-in-law how they would cook their food. The sister-in-law replied, "We will cook on one hearth, and all of you will eat." Everyone was happy with the sister-in-law and were very appreciative of her living with them. They were spending their days happily.

The festival of Diwali is celebrated after Dhanteras and Naraka Chaturdashi. The sister-in-law told her brothers, "On the day of Diwali, you all will wear new clothes." The brothers replied that they didn't have any new clothes. The sister-in-law said, "I have saved some money and bought new clothes for everyone." She then told everyone to clean their house.

The sister-in-law said, "Whatever you find today, bring it home." The youngest brother was playful and said, "If I find dirt, I will bring that too." The sister-in-law said, "Bring it home and wipe the doorstep with it." In the evening when everyone returned from work, the youngest brother brought a snake's slough. The sister-in-law told him to throw it on the roof. It turned out that the queen was bathing, and a vulture had stolen her necklace. When the vulture saw the slough on the roof, it dropped the necklace and flew away with the slough.

The king announced to the city that whoever found the queen's necklace would be rewarded with whatever they desired. When the potter's daughter-in-law saw the necklace on the roof, she was very happy and gave it to her father-in-law. She told him to go to the palace and give the necklace to the king and ask for a reward. She also told him to say, "Let only our house be lit with lamps on Diwali, or the king's house."

The father-in-law went to the palace and did as his daughter-in- law had instructed. The king agreed to the condition. On Naraka Chaturdashi, the father-in-law cleaned his house thoroughly and sat at the door. On the instructions of his daughter-in-law he told everyone who was going to go away for seven generations, and to those coming to come for seven generations.

In the evening, a dirty, ragged man with unkempt hair and

nails, and mud in his eyes, was walking out of the house. The father-in- law saw him and said, "Brother, where are you going? You are our life partner." The man who was dirt and muck of the house, replied, "Your daughter-in-law has made me miserable by continuously beating me with the broom. I can't stay here anymore." The father- in-law said, "Then go away for seven generations." The man replied, "Seven generations? Will go away for fourteen generations."

On the night of Diwali, there were lights only in the potter's house and in the king's house. A beautiful woman, adorned with jewellery, appeared at the potter's door.

The woman was actually Lakshmi herself. When she arrived at the potter's house, he was astonished. Lakshmi said, "We always reside in the king's house, but today, light is shining only in your house. That's why I have come here." The potter said, "Lakshmi ji, please come to our house for seven generations." Lakshmi replied, "Seven generations? I will come for fourteen generations?" From that day on, Lakshmi's abode became the potter's house for fourteen generations. As she was pleased with them, everyone was blessed with prosperity. As Lakshmi ji showered her blessings on potter's house, may she shower her blessings on everyone.

Second Story

Once, there was a Brahmin and his wife, both of whom were very poor. They sometimes had food, sometimes they went to sleep hungry. Once, it happened that for four days, the children didn't get anything to eat and were very weak due to hunger. The Brahmin's wife said, "Go and bring something to eat; it's not good to see the children crying." The Brahmin went straight to Lord Vishnu in heaven. Vishnu was playing a dice game with Lakshmi. The Brahmin went there and started saying, "Vishnu wins, Vishnu wins." Vishnu threw a handful of khichdi of munga and pearl grains. The Brahmin picked them up, tied them in a bundle, and was returning home. On the way, he met some children playing and they snatched the bundle from him. The sad Brahmin returned home empty-handed.

The next day, the Brahmin's wife again sent him. It was the fifth day. She said, "Bring something to eat, Brahmin." The Brahmin again went to Lord Vishnu and started saying, "Vishnu wins, Vishnu wins." Vishnu threw a ring. The Brahmin took the ring and was walking on the way when he reached the riverbank to drink water. The ring fell into the water and a fish swallowed it. The sad Brahmin returned home empty-handed and narrated the whole story to his wife.

On the third day, the Brahmin's wife again said, "Today, you must bring something." The Brahmin went to Vishnu and Lakshmi, who were playing dice on Sheshnag in the ocean of milk. The Brahmin started saying, "Vishnu wins, Vishnu wins." Vishnu gestured towards Lakshmi and prompted Brahmin to say, "Lakshmi wins, Lakshmi wins." The Brahmin continued saying, "Lakshmi wins, Lakshmi wins." Lakshmi became angry and said, "You always say Vishnu wins, Vishnu wins. You are saying Lakshmi wins today." Vishnu said, "I do give him, but he can't get it."

Lakshmi threw two coins towards him. The Brahmin took the coins and was walking back to his house. He saw a fish seller and bought all the fish with those two coins. The Brahmin returned home, and his wife was surprised. She said, "After so many days, you brought fish." There was no pan or spices at home. The Brahmin asked his wife to borrow them from the neighbors. The Brahmin's wife said, "The neighbors don't even talk to us cordially." After much persuasion, the Brahmin's wife went to the neighbors. The neighbors spoke very nicely to her and said, "Take spices, take a pan, take oil, and take whatever you need."

When the Brahmin's wife returned home, she cut the fish and a ring came out. At that time, the children brought khichdi made with munga and pearls, saying they had finished playing and didn't want it anymore. In this way, Lakshmi, by giving only two coins, returned all their wealth. When Lakshmi is pleased, everyone is blessed.

Lakshmi Ji Vrat Katha

Once upon a time, there was a Brahmin's daughter who was deeply devoted to Goddess Lakshmi. Every Saturday, she would observe a fast and visit a peepal tree to offer her prayers to the goddess. As she sat under the tree, she would hear a mysterious voice that would say, "I am Lakshmi, and you are the Brahmin's daughter. We are friends." This voice came to her every time she prayed, but she never spoke of it to anyone, quietly carrying on with her daily life.

One day, however, curiosity got the better of her, and she told her mother about the voice from the peepal tree. Her mother, intrigued and surprised, wanted to experience this for herself. On the next Saturday, the daughter and her mother went together to the peepal tree for the regular prayers. As they prayed, they both heard the same voice. Astonished, the mother spoke up, "If you are truly Lakshmi, appear before us so I can believe in your presence."

To their amazement, Goddess Lakshmi manifested from the peepal tree. Smiling upon the Brahmin's daughter, she said, "Come to my palace tomorrow." Overjoyed, the daughter and her mother returned home and excitedly shared the divine encounter with their neighbors. The news spread quickly, and the neighbors admired the Brahmin's daughter, eagerly sending her off to meet Lakshmi the following day.

The next day, the Brahmin's daughter went to Lakshmi's grand palace, where she was greeted with warmth and hospitality. Lakshmi fed her sumptuous meals and showered her with gifts of immense wealth before sending her back home. When she returned, the townspeople marveled at her newfound riches, saying, "She has become so wealthy!"

However, some began to whisper, "What will happen when the time comes to repay all this wealth?" These comments troubled the Brahmin's daughter, and she began to grow anxious. Her worries ate away at her, and day by day, she became thinner and more frail. Sensing her distress, Lakshmi appeared again and asked, "Why do you grow weaker when those blessed by me only prosper and flourish? You are my dear friend, yet you seem to be wasting away."

The Brahmin's daughter confessed her fears, explaining how the people's words had filled her with doubt. Pleased by her sincerity and friendship, Lakshmi reassured her, "I will visit your home and bring my blessings with me."

The Brahmin's daughter joyfully told her mother, and they began preparing their humble home to welcome the goddess. When Lakshmi arrived, she was accompanied by Ganesha, the god of wisdom and fortune, along with her nine treasures and twelve divine powers. It is said that wherever intelligence, wealth, treasures, and divine powers are present, Ganesha and Lakshmi will also reside.

As they approached the house, Lakshmi paused at the door and said, "I will not enter." After much persuasion from the Brahmin's daughter and the neighbors, she finally stepped inside. Before leaving, Lakshmi declared, "The nine treasures and twelve divine powers will remain in this house for seven generations. However, for the eighth generation, it will depend on their actions."

When Lakshmi departed, the Brahmin's daughter was astounded to find her house transformed. The door frames were golden, the doors were made of silver, and the entire home was filled with wealth and grains. Lakshmi, ever merciful to those who worship her with devotion, bestows happiness, prosperity, and blessings on those she favors.

Bhai Dooj

First Story

Lord Surya Narayana, the Sun God, had two wives: Chhaya and Sangya. Each wife had a son and a daughter. From Sangya, his first wife, were born Yama, the god of death, and Yamuna, the river goddess. Chhaya, his second wife, gave birth to Shani, the god of justice, and Tapti, the river goddess. However, the two families did not live in harmony. Chhaya, being a stepmother to Yama and Yamuna, mistreated them and favored her own children, Shani and Tapti. Her unfair treatment deeply hurt Yama, who eventually left the family home, retreating to Yamalok, the realm of the dead, to fulfill his duties of punishing wrongdoers.

Yamuna, heartbroken by her brother's departure, missed him dearly. She could not bear the separation, so she traveled to Vishrant Ghat in Mathura, a holy place, to perform penance in hopes of reuniting with her brother. She devoted herself to long and arduous prayers, seeking solace in the hope of Yama's return.

Meanwhile, time passed in Yamalok, and Yama, too, began to feel the absence of his sister. His longing to see Yamuna grew stronger, and he became determined to find her. Yama sent out his messengers to search for Yamuna across the universe, hoping to bring her back. However, despite their best efforts, the messengers failed to locate her and returned to Yama with the disappointing news.

Distressed by their failure, Yama decided to search for his sister himself. He descended to the mortal world and discovered that Yamuna was residing in Mathura, still engaged in her devout penance.

Overjoyed to see her brother, Yamuna welcomed Yama with great affection and love. She invited him to her home, where she lovingly fed him, made him sit comfortably on a mat, and applied a sacred tilak to his forehead, as a gesture of her devotion and respect.

Moved by Yamuna's devotion and sisterly love, Yama was immensely pleased. He offered her a boon, a divine blessing, and asked her to request anything she desired. In her happiness, Yamuna asked for a boon that would honor the bond between brothers and sisters. She wished that any sister who fed her brother, made him comfortable, and applied tilak to his forehead on that day would ensure her brother's eternal life and well-being.

Yama, touched by her selfless request, granted her the boon.

Additionally, Yamuna asked that any brother and sister who bathe together in the sacred Yamuna River on the day of Bhai Dooj, a festival dedicated to the brother-sister bond, should be blessed with a place in heaven. Yama, filled with admiration for his sister's love, readily agreed and fulfilled her wish.

Since that day, it is believed that taking a ritual bath in the Yamuna River on Bhai Dooj is an auspicious act that strengthens the bond between brothers and sisters. The festival has since been celebrated with great devotion, where sisters apply tilak to their brothers, feed them with love, and pray for their well-being, while brothers, in turn, vow to protect and cherish their sisters.

Second Story

There is another heartwarming story associated with Bhai Dooj, a festival that celebrates the bond between brothers and sisters. The tale revolves around a sister whose brother and husband had a disagreement. The husband, upset with his brother-in-law, was determined to prevent the customary Bhai Dooj ritual of tilak. On the morning of Bhai Dooj, he sat outside on a chair, right by the door, making sure that his wife's brother would not be able to enter the house. His intention was to stop the sister from applying the traditional tilak to her brother's forehead, a central part of the Bhai Dooj celebration.

The sister, deeply saddened by the situation, still prepared for the ritual with a heavy heart. She gathered all the necessary items—haldi (turmeric), roli (vermilion), and rice—and began grinding them to make the tilak paste. As she worked, tears filled her eyes, her sadness evident in every motion. She longed to see her brother and fulfill the sacred tradition, but it seemed impossible due to her husband's anger and the ongoing conflict between the two men.

The original version of the story has a humorous and symbolic twist. The brother eventually returned home, but in a disheveled state, looking like a dog that had fallen into a drain. When the sister saw him in this sorry state, she was initially startled and tried to shoo him away, not recognizing him. However, during this commotion, some of the tilak paste accidentally landed on her brother's forehead, fulfilling the ritual in an unexpected way. Even though it was not planned, the bond between the brother and sister was reaffirmed, showing that love and tradition cannot be easily broken.

In modern retellings, the ending is slightly different. Instead of arriving in a disheveled state, the brother arrives at his sister's home in a helicopter, a symbol of his grand return. The sister lovingly applies the tilak to his forehead, and the brother, in a playful mood, teases his brother-in-law, saying, "Look, I still got the tilak!" This lighthearted banter infuriates the husband, who demands to know how the tilak was applied while he was sitting at the door. The sister, quick on her feet, cleverly blames her husband, saying that he was there the whole time but failed to see anything.

This story teaches us an important lesson: no matter the obstacles or disagreements, the love between a brother and sister is unbreakable. Even when circumstances seem impossible, divine intervention, humor, or even fate will find a way to bring them together. Bhai Dooj, after all, celebrates the eternal bond that siblings share, proving that love will always triumph.

Third Story

There was once a wealthy man who had a daughter. When she reached marriageable age, he married her to a suitable groom who lived far away. Due to the distance, she couldn't visit her parents often. After her departure, the wealthy man was blessed with a son. The entire family was overjoyed.

Every year on Bhai Dooj, the boy would see the sisters applying tilak to their brothers. He would ask his mother if he could also go to his sister's house to get a tilak. His mother would dissuade him, saying that his sister lived far away and had a difficult temperament.

As the boy grew older, he became more determined and insisted on visiting his sister on Bhai Dooj. His mother, unable to resist his persistence, allowed him to go.

On his journey, he encountered many obstacles: rivers, mountains, and dense forests. First, he met a snake who threatened to bite him. The boy replied, "Let me get a tilak from my sister first, then you can bite me." The snake slithered away. Next, he encountered a lion in a dense forest. The boy said the same thing to the lion, and it too left him alone.

The boy continued his journey and encountered a river that threatened to carry him away. The boy replied, "Let me get a tilak from my sister first, then you can carry me away." The river agreed. He was about to reach his sister's house when a building's door started to fall. Again, the boy said the same thing, and the door stayed still.

After overcoming all these obstacles, the boy finally reached his sister's house. He saw her spinning yarn. To his surprise, she didn't greet him or show any joy. There's a belief that if a spinning thread breaks, it's considered unlucky for the brother.

The boy thought to himself, "My mother was right. My sister has a bad temper." He was about to leave when the thread suddenly joined back together. His sister ran towards him, hugged him, and expressed her happiness. She explained that she had been praying for his well-being, but the broken thread prevented her from getting up and welcoming him.

Overjoyed, she went to her neighbors to ask what they usually prepare for a loved one's arrival. The neighbors jokingly suggested swabbing the kitchen floor by ghee and cooking rice in sugar. The sister followed their advice, but the kitchen floor would not dry, and the rice didn't cook. The boy wondered what she was making. He was very hungry.

The sister went back to her neighbors, who laughed at her for taking their joke seriously. They told her to use cow dung to light the stove and cook the rice with milk. The sister followed their instructions and served the food to her brother with love.

After a few days had passed, the brother said he wanted to go home. The sister replied, "Let's leave at dawn, as the journey is long." At night, the sister woke up, ground flour, made laddus for the journey, and sent her brother off to sleep. In the morning, the children wanted to eat the laddus made for their uncle. When they opened the container, they saw that all the laddus were black and a snake's tail was sticking out of the grinder. The snake had been ground up in the dark of the night.

The sister was devastated, fearing that her brother might eat the poisonous laddus. She left the children in their cradle, left the cooking unattended, and ran out in search of her brother. Under a tree, she saw her brother sleeping, surrounded by crows and birds pecking at the laddus.

In a panic, she woke her brother up and asked if he had eaten any of the laddus. He replied that he hadn't. They thanked God for their brother's safety. The brother said to his sister, "How far will you go to protect me? There are many people who are after my life.

The sister replied, "Let's go home and tell me in detail about this." The brother narrated the entire story of journey. The sister decided to accompany her brother on the return journey. The sister convinced her brother to let her accompany him. She had not visited her parents in a long time. She entrusted her house to her neighbor and prepared for the journey, taking necessary supplies.

After traveling a short distance, the sister said, "I am thirsty." The brother replied, "I told you the journey would be difficult. Where can I find water?" The sister pointed to birds flying in the distance and said, "There must be water nearby. You sit here, and I'll go get some."

The sister went to fetch water. Despite her brother's protests, she went and returned with the water. As she was drinking, she saw the Yamadutas writing on a yamshila (stone). She asked, "Uncle what are you writing?"

The Yamadutas replied, "We usually don't tell anyone, but since you called us 'uncle,' we'll tell you. We are writing down the time of death for those who are the only son and brother of the only brother. At the time of his marriage, he will die because of a snake bite. The sister was heartbroken and asked if there was a solution. The Yamadutas said, "If you can find a potter's or washerwoman's daughter who has observed Bhai Dooj and Ekadashi vrats, give her blessings to your brother and start cursing him from right now. He might be saved."

The sister returned and started cursing her brother. Her brother was confused and asked, "What's wrong with you? Are you crazy?"

As they continued their journey, the gate of a fort was about to fall. The sister placed a brick under the gate, preventing it from falling. They continued their journey and encountered a snake that was about to bite her brother. She placed a cup of milk in front of the snake, and the snake drank it and left.

They walked a little further and encountered a lion. The sister scrubbed his back with a scrubber to soothe the lion, and it went away. They reached a river that was starting to flood. The sister placed her clothes and bangles on the river, and the flood subsided.

Finally, they reached their mother's house.

They walked a little further and encountered a lion. The sister used a fragrant herb to soothe the lion, and it went away. They reached a river that was about to flood. The sister placed her clothes and bangles on the river, and the flood subsided.

Finally, they reached their mother's house.

The brother said to his mother, "My sister has also come." When the sister arrived, she immediately befriended the washerwoman's and potter's daughters. She spent a lot of time at their houses, helping them with their work, which strengthened their friendship.

The time for the brother's wedding arrived. People said that the sister had gone crazy and should be locked in a room. The sister took her brother's turban and locked herself in the room. When it was time for the wedding procession to leave, everyone started searching for the brother's turban.

The sister shouted from the window, "I have the turban!" People opened the door, but the sister said, "Open the window, we'll come out through the window." As soon as they opened the door, the door fell. Everyone said, "This girl has supernatural powers."

The wedding procession started. The sister took her friends and followed the procession, shouting insults from a bullock cart. After traveling a distance, the procession stopped under a tree. The sister said, "Don't stop here." The procession moved a little further and stopped again. At that moment, the tree fell.

The wedding reached its destination. The groom arrived at the mandap. At that moment the sister asked the potter's daughter and the washerwoman's daughter to give her the fruits of their fasts and penance. They said, "How can we give you the fruits of our life long fasts and penance?" After much persuasion, they agreed to give her the fruits.

At that moment, a snake appeared in the mandap. The sister caught the snake, put it in her kurta, and sewed it up. Due to the power of her friends' fasts and penance, she had gained supernatural abilities. She saved her brother and blessed him with infinite happiness. Then, she returned to her mother's home.

The brother got married and brought his wife home. The sister told her mother to invite all the villagers for a gathering. She showed everyone the snake that had been trapped in her pocket. The sister said, "my mission is accomplished. I will go to my home now."

The brother's father-in-law gave them a cow as a gift. Everyone praised the sister for saving her brother's life and suggested giving the cow to her as a reward. The sister accepted the cow and left for her home.

When she arrived home, the cow started giving a lot of milk. This brought prosperity to her house. Her sister-in-law became jealous and told her husband that the cow belonged to her maternal home and should be returned. Despite everyone's attempts to persuade her, she refused to listen.

Finally, the brother went to his sister's house and reluctantly asked for the cow. His sister agreed, saying, "There's no big deal. Take the cow." When the cow returned to her brother's house, it stopped giving milk. It started excreting so much of dung that it became difficult to manage its large quantities.

The mother said, "Whatever is destined for someone will ultimately be theirs." The cow was returned to the sister, and the brother and sister's unbreakable bond continued forever. Just as they were bound by unconditional love, so may all brothers and sisters be united by love.

Fourth Story

Bhai Dooj, a festival celebrating the beautiful bond between brothers and sisters, is observed on the second day of the Kartik month in the Hindu calendar. This special occasion strengthens sibling relationships and is believed to bring blessings of longevity and well-being. One of the ancient traditions associated with Bhai Dooj is that brothers and sisters who bathe together in the sacred Yamuna River at Vishrant Ghat in Mathura will escape the clutches of death. Yama, the god of death, is said to personally escort them to heaven, sparing them from Yamalok, his domain.

On Bhai Dooj, the sister plays an important role in the rituals. She seats her brother on a raised platform, lovingly applies a tilak (a mark on the forehead made from a paste of roli and rice) to his forehead, and feeds him delicious food. The tilak is a symbol of her blessings for his long life, prosperity, and happiness. In return, the brother gives his sister gifts as a token of his love and gratitude, pledging to protect and care for her.

There is an interesting and ancient story that ties Bhai Dooj to the city of Mathura. Long ago, there was a noble king in Mathura, and he had a virtuous queen. The queen and her maid were very close friends. By coincidence, both women became pregnant around the same time. They made a pact: if one of them had a son and the other had a daughter, they would marry their children to each other. When the time came, the queen gave birth to a daughter, and the maid to a son. The maid's son grew up believing that he would one day marry the princess, since he was destined to become a prince.

However, as the princess grew older, she began to worry about the arrangement. She did not want to marry the maid's son and sought advice on how to avoid this. Finally, a wise man gave her an idea. He told her that the maid's son regularly went to Vishrant Ghat to sweep the area and then rest there. The wise man instructed the princess to bathe in the Yamuna River from Dhanteras (the first day of Diwali celebrations) to Bhai Dooj, and each day, after bathing, to apply a tilak on the maid's son—

starting with his toe, then his thigh, stomach, chest, and finally his forehead on the fifth day. By doing this, she could call him her brother and escape the marriage pact.

The princess was pleased with the suggestion and followed it meticulously. On Dhanteras, she woke up early, bathed in the Yamuna, and applied a tilak to the maid's son's toe. She made a parrot on a nearby tree her witness, asking it to repeat her actions. The next morning, the maid's son woke up surprised to see the tilak mark on his toe, and the parrot repeated what the princess had said. This continued for the next few days, with the tilak gradually moving higher on his body. On the fifth day, the princess boldly applied the tilak to his forehead, held his hand, and declared, "From today, you are my sworn brother, and I am your sworn sister."

This act sealed their bond as siblings, freeing her from the marital arrangement. The story also reinforces the traditional belief that siblings who bathe in the Yamuna River on Bhai Dooj will live a long and prosperous life. Bhai Dooj, thus, celebrates the sacred love and protective bond between brothers and sisters, ensuring happiness, peace, and longevity for both.

Chhath Puja: A Celebration of the Sun

Chhath Puja is a deeply revered and ancient Hindu festival, celebrated with immense devotion and gratitude toward the Sun God. It takes place a few days after Diwali, during the sixth day of the bright half of the Kartik month (usually in October or November). The festival is predominantly observed in the states of Bihar, Jharkhand, and Uttar Pradesh, as well as parts of eastern India, particularly in Nepal's Mithila region. Chhath Puja holds special significance for millions of devotees who celebrate it to honor the life-sustaining power of the Sun.

One of the unique aspects of Chhath Puja is its inclusivity. Unlike some religious festivals, Chhath Puja can be observed by anyone, irrespective of their religious background. This four-day-long festival requires a high degree of physical and mental discipline. Participants practice rigorous fasting, abstaining from even drinking water during certain phases, and perform elaborate rituals to express their deep reverence for the Sun. The festival is often referred to as a form of "Hatha Yoga," emphasizing the strict physical and mental discipline involved.

The ancient origins of Chhath Puja are found in Hindu scriptures, with mentions in both the Ramayana and the Mahabharata. According to the Skanda Purana, it is believed that it is sinful to eat without first offering water to the Sun God. The Sun and the Moon are considered direct deities, essential for maintaining the balance of nature. The rays of the Sun are vital for the production of food, flowers, and the sustenance of life on Earth. Offering water to the Sun during Chhath is a gesture of gratitude, acknowledging its crucial role in supporting life.

In addition to religious significance, there are scientific and Ayurvedic perspectives tied to the rituals of Chhath Puja. According to traditional Ayurvedic principles, offering water to the Sun, especially during the early hours of the morning, is believed to have numerous health benefits. As the water flows over one's head and down the body, it is thought to interact with the Sun's rays, which enhances intellectual abilities, strengthens the immune system, and revitalizes the body.

The legend behind Chhath Puja has roots in several Hindu stories. One such story recounts that when Sita Devi returned to Ayodhya after her 14-year exile with Lord Rama, she performed a Rajsuya Yagya as advised by sages. Sage Mugdal invited Rama and Sita to his ashram on the day of Chhath Puja, where Sita was instructed to worship the setting Sun and offer Arghya (water and flowers). She observed a strict fast for two days, in honor of the Sun God.

Another story links Chhath Puja to the Mahabharata. Kunti, mother of Karna, worshipped the Sun to seek blessings for her son, Karna, who was born as a result of her devotion to the Sun God. The ritual of bathing in a river at sunset and offering Arghya to the rising Sun is mentioned in the Atharva Veda, highlighting the festival's importance in Hinduism.

The Brahmavaivarta Purana also recounts a story of Manu Priyavrat and his wife Malini, who were childless. After the death of their newborn son, Malini sought divine intervention, and the daughter of Brahma blessed her, advising her to observe Chhath Puja. As a result, Malini and her people were blessed with happiness and prosperity, symbolizing the fulfillment of wishes and well-being through devotion.

Chhath Puja is a profound celebration of gratitude to the Sun, a powerful reminder of humanity's connection with nature, and a testament to faith, discipline, and devotion.

Short Stories
(Laghu Kathayen)

The Blind Man's Deeds

Once upon a time, Indra, the king of the gods, desired to find a truly worthy soul on Earth who deserved a place in heaven. To accomplish this, he sent two of his divine messengers on a mission. Their task was to search the Earth and find a person who exemplified the qualities of selflessness, goodness, and virtue.

The messengers set off, traveling across cities and villages, observing the deeds of countless people. One day, while walking down a dusty road, they encountered a blind man sitting by the roadside, carefully lighting a lamp. Puzzled by the sight, they approached him and asked, "You are blind and cannot see. What is the purpose of lighting a lamp when it serves no benefit to you?"

The blind man sat in silence for a moment, contemplating the question. Then, in a calm and gentle voice, he replied, "It is true that I am blind and unable to see the light of this lamp. However, others who walk this path can see. By lighting this lamp, I can help guide them and illuminate their way. Though I cannot benefit from the light, I know it will serve those who need it. That is my accomplishment."

The messengers were deeply moved by the blind man's response. His profound act of selflessness, doing good for others despite his own limitations, was a rare and noble quality. They returned to Indra and recounted the entire story.

Upon hearing of the blind man's actions, Indra was filled with admiration. Recognizing the man's pure heart and selfless deed,

Indra declared him worthy of a place in heaven. The blind man's simple yet powerful act of lighting a lamp to help others became a symbol of true virtue and generosity. His kindness illuminated not just the path of travelers but also the way to heaven, showing that selflessness is the greatest light of all.

The Power of Contentment

Once upon a time, there was a wealthy merchant who possessed vast riches. His fortune was so immense that he began to wonder just how much he truly owned. Eager to understand the full extent of his wealth, he summoned his accountant and asked him to carefully review all the financial records and report the total amount. After meticulously examining the accounts, the accountant informed him that his wealth was so abundant that it would comfortably provide for his descendants for seven generations.

Despite this reassuring news, the merchant felt troubled. His thoughts lingered on the future, and a nagging concern grew within him: "What about the eighth generation?" The idea that his descendants, so far into the future, might face hardship left him distressed. No amount of wealth seemed enough to calm his mind. Seeking peace, the merchant decided to consult a wise sage, hoping the sage would offer him guidance.

The merchant explained his worries to the sage, who listened patiently. After a moment of contemplation, the sage smiled and offered a simple piece of advice: "In this city, there is a poor old woman who struggles to make ends meet. Donate half a kilo of flour to her."

Surprised by the suggestion, the merchant thought to himself, "Just half a kilo of flour? Why not give her something more substantial?" In his mind, giving such a small amount seemed insignificant, so he decided to be more generous. The next day, the merchant brought an entire quintal of flour—a large, heavy sack—to the old woman's house.

When the old woman saw the enormous amount of flour, she was taken aback. "Child, I am just one person," she exclaimed. "How can I possibly use so much flour?"

The merchant kindly replied, "If you can't use it all today, you can keep the rest for tomorrow."

The old woman smiled and said, "Child, why should I worry about tomorrow when I have enough for today? Just as I have managed today, I will manage tomorrow as well."

Her words struck the merchant deeply. He realized that this poor old woman, who had so little, was completely content, living peacefully without worrying about the future. Meanwhile, he, a man of immense wealth, was consumed by anxiety about generations far beyond his own time. In that moment, the merchant understood that true happiness lies not in hoarding wealth, but in being content with what we have in the present.The merchant had learned a profound lesson: living in constant fear of future uncertainties only robs us of peace today. True happiness comes from contentment, not from endless accumulation.

Vikram Samvat

2072 years ago, the king of Ujjain, Bharatari, had a wife named Pingala, who was a stunning beauty. Pingala developed feelings for her brother-in-law, Vikramaditya, which he rejected. Hurt, Pingala devised a plan to frame Vikramaditya for misconduct. She convinced the king to exile Vikramaditya.

Vikramaditya found refuge in the ashram of a sage in the forest. In the same forest, an elderly couple lived. Impressed by their devotion, the Lord blessed them with a fruit. They felt that since they are already old, why not give it to the King Bhartari so that he can continue ruling his kingdom eternally. So they decided to offer this fruit to King Bharatari, hoping it would grant him eternal life and rule.

King Bharatari received the divine fruit and gave it to his queen. The queen, who was in love with an equestrian, gave the fruit to him. The equestrian, thinking he had no use for it, gave it to a courtesan. The courtesan, realizing her own sinful life, decided to offer the fruit to the king, hoping it would prolong his life and rule.

When the king received the fruit, he recognized it and questioned his queen about the fruit. The queen said that she has eaten the fruit. The enraged king showed her the fruit and immediately ordered her to leave the palace. The king himself renounced his worldly life.

In the forest where Vikramaditya resided, a prophecy was made: "Vikramaditya, rise and go rule your brother's kingdom." The Vikram Samvat calendar we use today was established by Vikramaditya 2072 years ago. The ability to predict future events, such as auspicious days for ceremonies and planetary positions, is a remarkable feat.

Ravana's Wisdom

In the epic battle between Rama and Ravana, the climax saw Rama emerging victorious, defeating the mighty king of Lanka, Ravana. As Ravana lay on the battlefield, nearing the end of his life, Rama, despite being his adversary, recognized the intelligence and wisdom that Ravana possessed. Turning to his brother, Lakshmana, Rama said, "Ravana, though our enemy, is a man of great intellect. There is much to learn from him. Before he dies, go and seek his wisdom."

Lakshmana approached the dying Ravana, standing beside his head, waiting for the great king to impart any knowledge or advice. However, Ravana remained silent, offering no words of wisdom. Disappointed, Lakshmana returned to Rama and informed him, "Ravana has not shared any wisdom with me."

Rama, a master of humility and understanding, asked Lakshmana a simple but insightful question: "Did you stand by his head or his feet?" Lakshmana responded, "I stood by his head, brother." Rama then advised, "To seek knowledge from someone as wise as Ravana, you must approach with humility. Go back and stand at his feet."

Following Rama's advice, Lakshmana returned to Ravana and humbly stood by his feet. Despite being gravely injured, Ravana, now recognizing Lakshmana's respect, began to share his wisdom, acknowledging the mistakes of his own life.

One of the most profound lessons Ravana imparted was, "In life, always prioritize good deeds over bad ones. I made the mistake of choosing the opposite path. Despite the immense power and gifts I earned through my austerities—such as the ability to produce fire without smoke, create fragrance in gold, purify seawater, and even build a staircase to heaven—I squandered these gifts on evil deeds. My actions ultimately led to my downfall, and now my end is near."

Ravana's words carried a powerful message, a warning against the destructive nature of evil actions. He revealed that all the power in the world means nothing when it is misused, and the consequences of one's choices are inescapable. His final lesson to Lakshmana and to the world was this: "Never postpone good deeds for tomorrow. Do them today, because tomorrow is uncertain."

In his dying moments, Ravana shared the universal truth that time waits for no one. The opportunity to do good should not be delayed, for life is unpredictable. This lesson from the fallen king remains timeless—a reminder that good deeds, not power or wealth, are the true measure of a meaningful life.

Rama and Sita's Separation

It is an eternal law of nature that one reaps what one sows, a principle that has governed human existence since time immemorial. This profound truth is reflected not only in daily life but also in the timeless stories passed down through the ages, particularly in the ancient scriptures of the Puranas.

One such story from the Puranas illustrates this principle vividly. In a time long ago, demons were wreaking havoc across the world, spreading fear and destruction. In an effort to escape their inevitable downfall, they sought refuge in the peaceful ashram of Bhrigu Rishi, a revered sage known for his wisdom and deep connection to the divine. The demons, knowing that Bhrigu Rishi's wife was renowned for her purity and compassion, pleaded with her for shelter.

Moved by their pleas, Bhrigu Rishi's wife offered them protection, despite their nefarious deeds. However, the gods, led by Lord Vishnu, were determined to put an end to the demons' reign of terror. They pursued the demons relentlessly, eventually reaching Bhrigu Rishi's ashram, where the demons were hiding. The gods demanded that Bhrigu Rishi's wife hand over the demons, but she refused. Out of her deep sense of compassion, she sheltered them, defying the will of the gods.

In a difficult and decisive moment, Lord Vishnu, who is responsible for maintaining cosmic order, decided that the demons must be destroyed, even if it meant sacrificing the life of

Bhrigu Rishi's wife. He intervened directly, leading to the death of the demons and the tragic death of the Rishi's wife.

When Bhrigu Rishi returned and discovered the sacrifice of his beloved wife, his heart was filled with grief. Using his divine powers, he revived her, but his pain and sorrow were immense. In his anguish, the Rishi cursed Lord Vishnu, saying that just as he had suffered the unbearable pain of separation from his wife, Lord Vishnu too would one day experience the same agony.

This curse was eventually fulfilled when Lord Vishnu took the form of Lord Rama, an incarnation that would later endure the heart- wrenching separation from his beloved wife, Sita, after she was abducted by the demon king Ravana. The curse of Bhrigu Rishi manifested in Lord Rama's life, reflecting the inevitable law of karma: even the divine must face the consequences of actions.

This story underscores the timeless principle that no one is exempt from the results of their actions. It teaches that all deeds, whether good or bad, will eventually come back to us, often in ways we least expect.

The Story of Dhruva

Long ago, there was a noble king named Uttanapada, known for his fairness and devotion to his people. His first queen, Suniti, was a virtuous and kind-hearted woman who treated everyone with fairness and grace. Together, they had a son named Dhruva. Suniti and Dhruva shared a peaceful, loving bond, and though their lives were modest, they were content.

One day, while out hunting, King Uttanapada came across a woman of extraordinary beauty named Suruchi. Captivated by her charm, the king fell deeply in love with her and decided to make her his second queen. However, Suruchi put forth a harsh condition: she would not enter the royal palace as long as Suniti, the first queen, remained there. Completely enchanted by Suruchi's beauty, the king agreed to her terms. As a result, he moved Suniti and Dhruva to a smaller, separate palace on the outskirts of the royal grounds, where they lived in relative isolation.

In time, Suruchi gave birth to a son named Uttama. Both Uttama and Dhruva grew up in their respective households, but while Uttama was surrounded by royal splendor, Dhruva lived a quieter, more humble life with his mother, away from the palace's luxuries.

One day, King Uttanapada was sitting outside the palace, and his son Uttama came and sat on his lap. Shortly afterward, Dhruva, who longed for his father's affection, also approached and tried to sit on the other side of his father's lap. Seeing this, Suruchi's heart filled with jealousy, and she sharply ordered Dhruva to get down. She told him that only her son, Uttama, had the right to sit on the king's lap, leaving young Dhruva heartbroken.

Confused and deeply hurt, Dhruva ran to his mother, Suniti, with a torrent of questions: "Who is my father? Why do we live away from the palace? Why does no one care about us?" Suniti, unable to offer satisfactory answers to these innocent yet profound questions, simply said, "You will be known not by birth or privilege but by your actions and achievements."

Determined to prove himself, the five-year-old Dhruva retreated into the dense forest. There, he engaged in severe penance and sought the guidance of sages and the revered Saptarishis. His unwavering devotion and determination soon attracted the attention of the gods, shaking even Indra's throne. The gods, deeply impressed by Dhruva's dedication, blessed him and declared him the foremost of all sages. They proclaimed that Dhruva would be the brightest star in the heavens, shining eternally, while other stars might fade with time.

Dhruva's only wish was to sit on his father's lap. Upon hearing of Dhruva's accomplishments and the divine blessings bestowed upon him, King Uttanapada was filled with immense pride. Overcome with joy, he declared, "From this day forward, I shall be known as Dhruva's father," and in a gesture of deep respect for his son, abdicated the throne. Dhruva was crowned the new king, ruling wisely and justly.

Dhruva's story became immortal, and he was granted the eternal blessing of shining as the North Star, guiding all who look to the heavens. His tale remains a testament to perseverance, humility, and the power of actions over privilege.

The Elephant and the Crocodile

God always hears the sincere prayers that emerge from the depths of one's heart. When someone is in extreme distress, their heartfelt cries for help reach the divine, and in those moments, God inevitably comes to their aid. One such story that beautifully illustrates this truth is the tale of the elephant and the crocodile, which serves as a testament to the power of faith and divine intervention.

Once, a herd of elephants gathered near a pond in the jungle to quench their thirst after a long journey. The elephants drank their fill and began to leave one by one. However, one elephant lingered by the pond, still thirsty and unaware of the danger lurking beneath the water's surface. Suddenly, a crocodile seized the elephant's leg in its powerful jaws, and a fierce struggle ensued between the two mighty creatures. The battle raged for hours, but the crocodile, being in its natural element, had the upper hand.

The elephant, unable to free itself, grew exhausted and began to sink deeper into the water. Only its trunk remained above the surface, desperately trying to breathe. In this moment of dire distress, with no hope in sight, the elephant cried out to God, "Oh Hari! Oh Hari!"

In Vaikuntha, Lord Vishnu, who was resting in the cosmic ocean of milk, heard the elephant's sincere cry for help. Without a moment's hesitation, the Lord mounted his divine bird, Garuda, and flew swiftly to the scene of the struggle. Upon arriving, Lord

Vishnu unleashed his divine weapon, the Sudarshana Chakra, striking down the crocodile and freeing the elephant from its clutches.

As the crocodile lay dying, it questioned the Lord, "Why did you kill me? We were both engaged in the same battle. Why did you choose to save the elephant and not me?"

Lord Vishnu calmly replied, "The elephant called out to me with pure faith and sincerity. You did not. That is why I came to its aid and vanquished you."

This story highlights the importance of true faith and devotion. God responds to the sincere calls of those who turn to Him in times of need, extending His grace and protection to those who trust in Him completely.

The Bliss of Renunciation

In ancient times, the revered Saint Ramananda lived on the outskirts of a bustling city, accompanied by his devoted disciples. Among them, Gautam held a special place in the saint's heart. The citizens of the city deeply admired Ramananda and his followers, often showering them with generous donations and heartfelt gifts, grateful for their spiritual guidance and wisdom.

One day, after much contemplation, Ramananda addressed his disciples with a thought-provoking proposition: "We have stayed in this city for quite some time. It is now time for us to embark on a journey to another place." Gautam, however, expressed his reluctance to leave the comforts of their current abode. He argued, "Master, we are well-known here, and we receive ample offerings. Why would we choose to leave such a bountiful place?"

Ramananda, embodying the essence of a true ascetic, responded with gentle conviction, "What do we truly need with wealth and material possessions? Our real path lies in the practice of renunciation." Despite his master's wisdom, Gautam remained unconvinced, and in a moment of weakness, he secretly hid a few coins in his pouch, unwilling to let go of even a small token of wealth.

As they journeyed onward, the group reached the banks of a wide river. As night began to fall, they encountered a ferryman who demanded two coins to transport them across. Being a saint, Ramananda had no money to offer, and the growing darkness created an unsettling atmosphere. The ferryman, sensing the danger of lingering by the river at night, urged them to seek another means of passage.

Seeing his beloved teacher in distress, Gautam's heart stirred with compassion. Overcome by the urgency of the situation, he retrieved the hidden coins from his pouch and offered them to the ferryman. "Here," he said, "these coins will help us cross safely."

As they made their way across the river, Gautam turned to Ramananda, hoping to justify his earlier actions. "Master, look! These coins I once clung to have now helped us in this moment of need."

Ramananda smiled warmly and replied, "Ah, my dear Gautam, it was only when you relinquished your attachment to the coins that our dilemma was resolved. True happiness and freedom lie in renunciation, not in clinging to worldly possessions."

This experience imparted a profound lesson to Gautam and the other disciples, reinforcing the notion that true contentment comes from letting go and embracing a life of simplicity and spiritual fulfillment.

Ramshalaka

Ramshalaka is a unique and fascinating tool embedded in the *Ram Charit Manas,* composed by the revered poet-saint Tulsidas. It is not just a poetic verse but also serves as a form of ancient divination used by devotees to seek guidance from the divine. Let's explore its importance, significance, meaning, and usefulnes.

Meaning of Ramshalaka

Ramshalaka is essentially a grid made up of squares, each containing a letter from the *Ram Charit Manas.* This grid forms 15 squares horizontally and 15 vertically, creating a total of 225 smaller squares. Each letter corresponds to a specific couplet or stanza from the epic. The Ramshalaka grid is associated with predictive verses from the *Ram Charit Manas* and is used to gain insights or guidance during times of confusion, uncertainty, or important decision-making. It is believed that the couplet or stanza revealed through this process carries divine wisdom and can help resolve dilemmas by interpreting the words of Lord Rama.

Importance of Ramshalaka

The Ramshalaka is of great spiritual significance to devotees of Lord Rama. It is seen as a bridge between the mortal world and the divine wisdom of the Lord, enabling individuals to access his guidance when faced with uncertainty. As a tool of divination, it allows people to approach Lord Rama with their troubles or doubts and receive direction in accordance with his teachings. For devout followers, this act is more than seeking fortune—it is about reinforcing their faith and connecting with the larger truths embedded in the *Ramayana*.

The process of consulting the Ramshalaka is carried out with a reverent mind and heart. One must meditate on Lord Rama and ask a question with sincerity. Then, by picking a random number or square in the grid, the corresponding verse offers guidance believed to come directly from the divine.

Significance in Ram Charit Manas

The *Ram Charit Manas* is more than just a retelling of the *Ramayana*. It is a spiritual and moral compass that has guided millions of Hindus for centuries. Ramshalaka, found within this sacred text, symbolizes the interplay of destiny and divine will. The verses drawn from the Ramshalaka grid are considered the Lord's response to the devotee's query, much like an oracle.

The use of Ramshalaka reinforces the belief that answers to life's challenges lie in ancient scriptures. It is believed that no random choice made by an individual is truly random, but rather part of a divine plan. The stanza one chooses reflects the nature of their situation, the resolution they seek, or the guidance that Lord Rama wishes to provide. In this way, the Ramshalaka becomes a divine tool of instruction and insight.

Usefulness of Ramshalaka

Ramshalaka offers several layers of usefulness:

- **Guidance**: People often find themselves in moments of indecision where traditional logic or reasoning seems inadequate. Ramshalaka serves as a way to access divine wisdom, which can help clarify one's path.

- **Spiritual Reinforcement**: Engaging with the Ramshalaka is a devotional exercise. It strengthens one's connection with Lord Rama, bringing comfort in the thought that the divine is present and guiding them.
- **Psychological Support**: Often, the verses chosen by consulting Ramshalaka are interpreted in ways that provide peace of mind, resolve worries, and give strength to the individual to face challenges. It acts as a psychological anchor for those who believe in its power.
- **Faith and Devotion**: For believers, the use of Ramshalaka is an affirmation of their faith. The act of seeking answers through Lord Rama's words instills a sense of reverence and reinforces trust in divine guidance.

Conclusion

The Ramshalaka is much more than a simple grid of letters—it is a profound expression of faith in the divine providence of Lord Rama. It bridges the material and spiritual worlds, allowing devotees to seek wisdom from ancient scriptures during times of need. Its significance lies not just in its predictive value but in its ability to reassure and comfort believers, encouraging them to live with faith, humility, and trust in the divine plan. Through Ramshalaka, the teachings of the Ram Charit Manas continue to guide generations, helping people navigate life's challenges with clarity and grace.

We are including the following chapter on Ramshalaka Prashnavali in Hindi for clarity and better understanding and at the same time paving the way for using this Ramshalaka effectively and easily whenever the need arises. This has been borrowed with gratitude from Ram Charit Manas by Goswami Tulsi Das.

Ramshalaka Chapter in Hindi

रामशलाका-प्रश्नावली

(साभार - रामचरित मानस से)

मानसानुरागी महानुभावों को श्रीरामशलाका-प्रश्नावली का विशेष परिचय देने की कोई आवश्यकता नहीं प्रतीत होती। उसकी महत्ता एवं उपयोगिता से प्राय: सभी मानस प्रेमी परिचित होंगे। अत: नीचे उसका स्वरुपमात्र अंकित करके उससे प्रश्नोत्तर निकालने की विधि तथा उसके उत्तर-फलों का उल्लेख कर दिया जाता है। श्रीरामशलाका-प्रश्नावली का स्वरुप इस प्रकार है-

सु	प्र	उ	बि	हो	मु	ग	ब	सु	नु	बि	घ	धि	इ	द
र	रू	फ	सि	सि	रहिं	बस	हि	मं	ल	न	ल	य	न	अं
सुज	सो	ग	सु	कु	म	स	ग	त	न	इ	ल	धा	बे	नो
त्य	र	न	कु	जो	म	रि	र	र	अ	की	हो	सं	रा	य
पु	सु	थ	सी	जे	इ	ग	म*	सं	क	रे	हो	स	स	नि
त	र	त	र	स	हुँ	ह	ब	ब	प	चि	स	हिं	स	तु
म	का	ा	र	र	म	मि	मी	म्हा	ा	जा	हू	हीं	ा	ा
ता	रा	रे	री	ह्र	का	फ	खा	जू	ई	र	रा	पू	द	ल
नि	को	जो	गो	न	मु	जि	यँ	ने	मनि	क	ज	प	स	ल
हि	रा	मि	स	रि	ग	द	न्मु	ख	म	खि	जि	म	त	जं
सिं	ख	नु	न	को	मि	निज	र्क	ग	धु	ध	सु	का	स	र
गु	ब	म	अ	रि	नि	म	ल	ा	न	ढ़	ती	न	क	भ
ना	पु	व	अ	ा	र	ल	ा	ए	तु	र	न	नु	वै	थ
सि	हुँ	सु	म्ह	रा	र	स	स	र	त	न	ख	ा	ज	ा
र	ा	ा	ला	धी	ा	री	ा	हू	हीं	खा	जू	ई	रा	रे

दोहा - जबहिं पृच्छक अंक पर', अँगुली को धरि देत।
ताके अगिले अंक ते, नवमाक्षर गनि लेत।।
ऊपर को ऊपर लिखे, नीचे निम्न लिखेत।
रामशलाका प्रश्न यह, यथा उचित फल देत।।

विधि

इस रामशलाका-प्रश्नावली के द्वारा जिस किसी को जब कभी अपने अभीष्ट प्रश्न का उत्तर प्राप्त करने की इच्छा हो तो सर्वप्रथम उस व्यक्ति को भगवान् श्रीरामचन्द्रजी का ध्यान करना चाहिये। तदनन्तर श्रृद्धा-विश्वासपूर्वक मन से अभीष्ट प्रश्न का चिन्तन करते हुए प्रश्नावली के मनचाहे कोष्ठक में अँगुली या कोई शलाका रख देना चाहिये और उस कोष्ठक में जो अक्षर हो उसे अलग किसी कोरे कागज या स्लेट पर लिख लेना चाहिये। प्रश्नावली के कोष्ठक पर भी ऐसा कोई निशान लगा देना चाहिये जिससे न तो प्रश्नावली गन्दी हो और न प्रश्नोत्तर प्राप्त होने तक वह कोष्ठक भूल जाए। अब जिस कोष्ठक का अक्षर लिख लिया गया है उससे आगे बढ़ना चाहिये तथा उसके नवें कोष्ठक में जो अक्षर पड़े उसे भी लिख लेना चाहिये। इस प्रकार प्रति नवें अक्षर के नवें अक्षर को क्रम से लिखते जाना चाहिये और तब तक लिखते जाना चाहिये, जबतक उसी पहले कोष्ठक के अक्षर तक अँगुली अथवा शलाका न पहुँच जाय। पहले कोष्ठक का अक्षर जिस कोष्ठक के अक्षर से नवाँ पड़ेगा, वहाँ तक पहुँचते-पहुँचते एक चौपाई पूरी हो जायगी, जो प्रश्नकर्त्ता के अभीष्ट प्रश्न का उत्तर होगी। यहाँ इस बात का ध्यान रखना चाहिये कि किसी-किसी कोष्ठक में केवल 'आ' की मात्रा (ा) और किसी-किसी कोष्ठक में दो-दो अक्षर हैं। अत: गिनते समय न तो मात्रा वाले कोष्ठक को छोड़ देना चाहिये और न दो अक्षरों वाले

कोष्ठक को दो बार गिनना चाहिये। जहाँ मात्रा का कोष्ठक आवे वहाँ पूर्वलिखित अक्षर के आगे मात्रा लिख लेना चाहिये और जहाँ दो अक्षरों वाला कोष्ठक आवे वहाँ दोनों अक्षर एक साथ लिख लेना चाहिये।

अब उदाहरण के तौर पर इस रामशलाका-प्रश्नावली से किसी प्रश्न के उत्तर में एक चौपाई निकाल दी जाती है। पाठक ध्यान से देखें। किसी ने भगवान् श्रीरामचन्द्रजी का ध्यान और अपने प्रश्न का चिन्तन करते हुए यदि प्रश्नावली के* इस चिहन से संयुक्त 'म' वाले कोष्ठक में अँगुली या शलाका रखा और वह ऊपर बताये क्रम के अनुसार अक्षरों को गिन-गिनकर लिखता गया तो उत्तर स्वरुप यह चौपाई बन जायगी:

हो इ हि सो इ जो रा म* र चि रा खा।
को क रि त र्क ब ढ़ा वै सा खा।।

यह चौपाई बालकाण्डान्तर्गत शिव और पार्वती के संवाद में है। प्रश्नकर्त्ता को इस उत्तर स्वरुप चौपाई से यह आशय निकलना चाहिये कि कार्य होने में सन्देह है, अत: उसे भगवान् पर छोड़ देना श्रेयस्कर है।

इस चौपाई के अतिरिक्त श्रीरामशलाका-प्रश्नावली से आठ चौपाइयाँ और बनती हैं, उन सबका स्थान और फलसहित उल्लेख नीचे किया जाता है। कुल नौ चौपाइयाँ हैं-

१. सुनु सिय सत्य असीस हमारी। पूजिहि मन कामना तुम्हारी।।
स्थान: यह चौपाई बालकाण्ड में श्रीसीताजी के गौरी पूजन के प्रसंग में है। गौरी जी ने श्रीसीताजी को आर्शीवाद दिया है।
फल: प्रश्नकर्त्ता का प्रश्न उत्तम है, कार्य सिद्ध होगा।

२. प्रबिसि नगर कीजे सब काजा। हृदयँ राखि कोसलपुर राजा।।
स्थान: यह चौपाई सुन्दरकाण्ड में हनुमान्‌जी के लंका में प्रवेश करने के समय की है।
फल: भगवान् का स्मरण करके कार्यारम्भ करो, सफलता मिलेगी।

३. उघरहिं अंत न होइ निबाहू। कालनेमि जिमि रावन राहू।।
स्थान: यह चौपाई बालकाण्ड के आरम्भ में सत्संग-वर्णन के प्रसंग में है।
फल: इस कार्य में भलाई नहीं है। कार्य की सफलता में सन्देह है।

४. बिधि बस सुजन कुसंगत परहीं।
फनि मनि सम निज गुन अनुसरहीं।।
स्थान: यह चौपाई बालकाण्ड के आरम्भ में ही सत्संग-वर्णन के प्रसंग की है।
फल: खोटे मनुष्यों का संग छोड़ दो। कार्य पूर्ण होने में सन्देह है।

५. मुद मंगलमय संत समाजू। जो जग जंगम तीरथराजू।।
स्थान: यह चौपाई बालकाण्ड में संत-समाजरुपी तीर्थ के वर्णन में है।
फल: प्रश्न उत्तम है। कार्य सिद्ध होगा।

६. गरल सुधा रिपु करहिं मिताई। गोपद सिंधु अनल सितलाई।।
स्थान: यह चौपाई श्रीहनुमान्‌जी के लंका में प्रवेश करने के समय की है।
फल: प्रश्न बहुत श्रेष्ठ है। कार्य सफल होगा।

७. बरून कुबेर सुरेस समीरा। रन सन्मुख धरि काहुँ न धीरा।।
स्थान: यह चौपाई लंकाकाण्ड में रावण की मृत्यु के पश्चात् मन्दोदरी के विलाप के प्रसंग में है।
फल: कार्य पूर्ण होने में सन्देह है।

८. सुफल मनोरथ होहुँ तुम्हारे। रामु लखनु सुनि भए सुखारे।।
स्थान: यह चौपाई बालकाण्ड में पुष्पवाटिका से पुष्प लाने पर विश्वामित्रजी का आशीर्वाद है।
फल: प्रश्न बहुत उत्तम है। कार्य सिद्ध होगा।

इस प्रकार रामशलाका-प्रश्नावली से कुल नौ चौपाइयाँ बनती हैं, जिनमें सभी प्रकार के प्रश्नों के उत्तराशय सन्निहित हैं।

Reviews

I deeply appreciate the book, *India's Festivals: A Trove of Folklore and Anecdotes*, by Dr. Anupam Varma and Mrs. Shubhra Varma. This beautifully narrated collection highlights the cultural significance of our festivals through engaging stories and moral lessons.

Personally, it evokes fond memories of my grandmother recounting tales of Dussehra, Diwali, Holi, Makar Sankranti, Shivaratri, and the special five stories of Karvachauth. These cherished tales, though fragmented over the years, are now preserved for me to pass on to my children.

The book's detailed storytelling and vibrant illustrations capture the essence and energy of our festivals, making it both interesting and fun to read. I am sincerely grateful for this treasure that keeps my childhood traditions and cultural heritage alive.

Tanuj Bartar
Director,
Paragon Instrumentation Pvt. Ltd., Roorkee

****

I am honored to introduce *India's Festivals: A Treasure Trove of Folklore & Anecdote*, authored by the distinguished Dr. Anupam Varma and Mrs. Shubhra Varma. Rooted in Sanatan Dharma—the world's oldest spiritual tradition—India was once a global center of knowledge and culture. However, centuries of invasions inflicted great damage on our heritage, replacing much of the ancient Vedic system with foreign practices. Consequently, many in our younger generation know little of our cultural roots.

In *India's Festivals*, the authors beautifully uncover the stories, meaning, and values behind India's vibrant festivals, melas, and cultural symbols. Each celebration holds a timeless message for society, reminding us of our traditions' enduring relevance. This book is a valuable resource, particularly for young readers, and I am confident it will inspire a deeper appreciation of Sanatan heritage. My heartfelt congratulations to the authors.

Dr. Rajan Pradhan, M.D.
Medicos, Delhi

****

India is a country of festivals and festivities. This book on "India's Festivals" is unique and deserves to be treasured in every Indian house. It is informative for both children and grandparents alike as it is a valuable resource for understanding the stories behind India's festivals and fastings. It is so interesting and educative that once I started reading it, I finished it in one breadth. Festivals like Holi, Deewali, Janmashtami, Chath and many others are observed both with piousness as well as festivity. The authors describe vividly the story behind these festivals in a lucid language. I found these stories very interesting. Though these are ancient, they are still relevant having an eternal appeal. The four different stories of Bhai Dooj is quite fascinating not to speak of other stories like Krishna Janmastami, Navratri, Shivaratri, Ganesh Chaturthi among others. Everyone need to go through the book which is a treasure trove of wisdom.

Arun Sahay
CEO, Fore Academy
Former Chairman & Managing Director
Scooters India Limited

****

My earliest memories of childhood are listening to stories from my grandparents and elderly relatives when we used to go for our annual vacations, and those memories and emotions are priceless. Every good story also deserves an eloquent storyteller and that's exactly what this book is : an excellent narration of stories that are attached to our traditions and festivals, that are not only intriguing but also gives an excellent perspective of why these festivals have survived over centuries. This is an excellent read and thank you Dr. Anupam Verma sir for penning these stories down which are at a risk of being forgotten

Sujay Bhattacharya
Senior Vice President
NTT Data

****